Never Stop Walking

THE Life AND
Spirit OF Saint
Alphonsus
Liguori

Never Stop Walking

THE Life AND Spirit OF Saint Alphonsus Liguori

SISTER NANCY FEARON, IHM

Provided you do not stop walking,
sooner or later you will reach the journey's end.

Saint Alphonsus to
Sr. Brianna Carafa,
August 4, 1771

Liguori Publications
Liguori, Missouri

Library of Congress Cataloging-in-Publication Data
Fearon, Nancy.
    Never stop walking : the life and spirit of Saint Alphonsus Liguori / Sister
Nancy Fearon.
        p. cm.
    Originally published: Monroe Mich.: Sisters, Servants of the Immaculate
Heart of Mary, c1977.
    Includes bibliographical references (p.).
    ISBN 0-89243-928-9 (pbk.)
    1. Liguori, Alfonso Maria de', Saint, 1696–1787. 2. Spirituality—Catho-
lic Church—History of doctrines—18th century. 3. Catholic Church—Doc-
trines—History—18th centuty. I Title
BX4700.L6F4   1996
271'.6402—dc20
[B]   96-13491

Printed in the United States of America
00 99 98 97 96   5 4 3 2 1

Cover design by Wendy Barnes

One Liguori Drive • Liguori, MO 63057-9999 • (314) 464-2500
LIGUORI
PUBLICATIONS

For Margaret,
whose search for the spirit
was the beginning of it all

NEVER STOP WALKING IS NOT THE BIOGRAPHY of a saint. It is, instead, an effort to trace the special charism that gradually unfolded in the life of one man in the history of the Church. It attempts to search out and focus on the seven key stages in his life as he was forced to wrestle with the conflicting desires he found within his own heart, and the effect these struggles had on his own understanding of his mission within the Church.

Alphonsus' understanding of this mission had meaning far beyond the boundaries of his own life in the Spirit. As founder of the Redemptorist congregation, he left his own mark on the corporate charism that shaped not only this original foundation, but also the Rule of the Redemptoristine Sisters, and later in history on the Sisters, Servants of the Immaculate Heart of Mary, founded by the Redemptorist, Rev. Louis Florent Gillet.

Whether or not we are impressed with the career of Saint Alphonsus Liguori, Doctor of the Church, does not really matter now. When debates over doctrines and devotions are set aside, we are left with a man who struggled throughout a lifetime to be faithful to the call of the Spirit within him to live the gospel as it revealed itself in his own times.

Contents

CHAPTER 1

Christian Layman

It was a warm September in Marianella. Flies swarmed over the shiny fish piled high at many stalls in the small piazza, in spite of the efforts of solitary squatting women who tried to keep the air circulating over their offerings of "frutta de mare." The year was 1696 and the fortunes of the Liguori family were not what they once had been. Don Joseph de Liguori, Captain of the Royal Galleys, was still a respected member of the lesser Neopolitan nobility; but the ancient family of Liguori looked back with pride to ancestors four centuries removed. Other bearers of the name Liguori had boasted far greater power; still others had accumulated far greater wealth.

But today Don Joseph was strangely satisfied with his lot in life. The warm Mediterranean sun greeted him as he emerged from the village church and followed him as he walked resolutely past the mounds of grape clusters and new olives. Donna Anna, his cherished wife, was soon to deliver his first son. It would be a son; he was sure of it.

Before this Thursday, the twenty-seventh day of September, had ended, a son was indeed born to Don Joseph. Two days later in the Church of the Queen of Virgins in nearby Naples, the boy was baptized Alphonsus Maria Antony John Francis Cosmos Damien Michael Gaspard Liguori.[1]

The future of Alphonsus took shape in the imagination of Don Joseph even before the day of his baptism. He would receive the finest liberal education money and parental supervision could provide in preparation for a career at court. He would marry well and transmit the name of Liguori with honor. Donna Anna sometimes shared his dreams.

Like many Italian mothers before and after her, Donna Anna sought to soften the sometimes overpowering influence of her husband on the small boy. Complementing rather than canceling the effect of his sometimes harsh manner, she gave Alphonsus the beginnings of a gift he was to foster all his life. Donna Anna taught Alphonsus the power of prayer. Later he would refine the gift, of course, yielding to the Spirit that moved his heart and his spirit, but the outlines would not change substantially.

Prayer, for Alphonsus became the loom of his life; and the same lessons were shared by the three brothers and three sisters who were later born to the Liguori family. Benedict later became novice master of the monks at Monte Cassino; Cajetan became a Neopolitan priest; Mary Aloisa and Mariana entered the convent of Saint Jerome at Naples. Hercules would later assume the inheritance of Alphonsus; and Teresina, the youngest daughter, later became the Duchess of Prezenzano.

Many years later, while Bishop of Saint Agata, Alphonsus would write:

> If there was any good in me in my childhood, I owe it entirely to my mother's care. My father was almost continually at sea and could not devote himself as he would have wished to the education of his children, so the whole responsibility fell upon my mother.[2]

When he was old enough to receive the sacrament of Penance for the first time, Donna Anna entrusted his spiritual guidance to her relative and spiritual director, Father Thomas Pagano, an Oratorian priest. Father Pagano's own spirituality flowed from the sources of the spirit of his Community.[3] The following words of Jean-Jacques Olier find a later echo in many places in the writings of Alphonsus: "To be a complete Christian you must share in all the mysteries of Jesus Christ."[4]

As the Spirit gradually formed the spirit of Alphonsus over a period of many years, three themes would surface again and again.

Drawing from hundreds of sources, Alphonsus would sharpen his focus on them in countless ways.

(1) the spirit of simplicity fostered by reflection on the mystery of the Incarnation
(2) the spirit of deep prayer fed by reflection on Christ's own life of prayer and on his Eucharistic life
(3) the spirit of sacrificial love growing out of a growing understanding of the mystery of Redemption[5]

At nine, Alphonsus was admitted to a group of young noblemen attached to the Oratory of which Father Pagano was Superior.[6] Besides sharing in spiritual exercises, the young boys joined their teachers on a number of short trips.

But as Alphonsus neared adolescence, Don Joseph assumed greater control of his education. Rather than arrange for a boarding school, his father chose to have him educated in his own home. The daily schedule would stagger many students today. Besides the mastery of Italian, his classical teacher and principal tutor, Father Dominic Buonaccio, taught him Latin, Greek, and French. Science and mathematics also formed part of his father's carefully constructed curriculum.[7]

From early childhood his father had provided lessons in drawing, painting, and architecture. Alphonsus later used the technical skills learned from this period in the creation of a large number of oil paintings and statues that were placed in different Redemptorist houses. Their simplicity stands in marked contrast to the overly ornate style of the period.

But music was Don Joseph's driving passion,[8] and Alphonsus, his favorite son, bore the burden of his father's ambition. Three hours a day Alphonsus was commanded to practice at the keyboard of the tiny harpsichord in the music room. If his father were called away during the practice session, he would calmly lock the door on Alphonsus and the music teacher and proceed with his business.

By the age of fourteen, Alphonsus had already undertaken at least an introductory study of scholastic philosophy and logic. He then turned to a study of both civil and canon law. The maze of statutes and overlapping codes that plagued the kingdom of Naples was unusual even for an Italian state,[9] since the kingdom had been occupied by the Greeks, Romans, and Byzantines even before the dawn of modern history. More recent occupations of Naples had been accomplished by both the Spanish and French. The bewildering collection of legal statutes patched together by various conquerors had never been codified. So to undertake the study of such a maze was quite a task for an adolescent.

The one recreation permitted in the schedule drawn up for Alphonsus by his father during this period was a single hour a day spent at the home of a friend, Don Balthasar Cito, where several young men would gather for a game of cards. One night Alphonsus became so absorbed in the game that he forgot the time limit and returned home later than usual only to find a wrathful father standing over his study table which had been strewn with playing cards.[10] The incident did nothing to strengthen the bonds between the two.

On January 21, 1713, four years before the legal age for admission of doctoral candidates, Alphonsus, by faculty dispensation, took his examination for the degree of Doctor of Law. After passing with honors, the relatively short young boy was invested in a judicial robe. His later description of the event reveals some of his sensitivity about his height: "They had decked me out in a long robe that trailed under my feet and made everybody laugh...."[11]

One of the early biographers of Alphonsus, A. P. Rispoli, contends that Alphonsus drew up a set of rules to guide his life as a lawyer when he first received his degree.[12] They are summarized as follows:

(1) no lawyer should ever undertake an unjust cause
(2) he shall not defend even a just cause by unjust means
(3) he is bound to study thoroughly the evidence with as much care as though his own interest were at stake
(4) he should ask the help of God, the protector of justice
(5) a lawyer should not take charge of matters which are beyond his strength or talent
(6) when a lawyer, through delay or negligence, loses his case or injures his client, he is bound to make compensation

Alphonsus never lost a case during the eight years he practiced law, in spite of his refusal to haggle over a decision.[13] If Rispoli's recording of the early resolutions is correct, we might attribute part of this record to his decision never to plead a case that exceeded his talents.

Meanwhile, in the social world in which his family moved, Alphonsus was considered an extremely eligible bachelor. Well-born, accomplished, and increasingly successful, the eldest Liguori son was also, under Neopolitan law, heir to the entire family estate. By the time he was twenty, he moved freely in "better circles." Encouraged by Don Joseph, who had long been occupied in deciding on an appropriate match for the rising lawyer, Alphonsus devoted an ever-increasing portion of his time to hunting, and to attending concerts and baroque operas.[14] His appearance could also be counted on at every party that was considered worthy of attention.

Several mothers and daughters, conscious of his escalating success and aware also of the regard in which the family was held by the reigning monarchs, showered him with attention. The whirl of activity after such a confined adolescence was not unwelcome to the young lawyer. He was rich, successful, popular in the right circles, and able to manage a life that many regarded as highly Christian. The future seemed to hold everything a young man could hope for in this life. But events were not as cloudless as they might seem.

Two years after passing his examination, Alphonsus had transferred from the Confraternity to which he had belonged for nine years to the Society of Doctors, also moderated by his boyhood director, Father Thomas Pagano. Besides attending weekly meetings, members committed themselves to a life of prayer and Christian service. Each week they were to visit a hospital to give comfort to the sick. Alphonsus chose the Hospital of the Incurables[15] where he did more than make an appearance among those who had abandoned all hope. Moved by the suffering he saw there, the young lawyer could not confine himself to weekly visits. Whenever he found a few hours not committed elsewhere, he returned to the incurables. Overcoming a natural repugnance to the stench and filth that surrounded the patients, he performed tasks usually assigned to slaves or servants drawn from the lowest classes. He gently changed bandages reeking with the odor of advanced skin cancers, cleansed festering wounds, bathed and fed many patients, and tried to bring a small measure of hope to those who had been abandoned by society to die as quietly as possible. For a young man raised in a household that employed several servants and slaves, the tasks did not come naturally. Death was all around him and its odor clung to him long after he returned to another world, a world in which he was not servant but master.

During Holy Week each year both Don Joseph and Alphonsus made a retreat conducted either by the Jesuits or by the Vincentians,[16] and each year the young man grew more restless. Unaware of the conflict churning within his son's heart, Don Joseph continued negotiations for a suitable marriage for his son. And, after sifting several possibilities, his favor settled on the daughter of Don Francis, Prince of Presiccio. Donna Teresa, who was only sixteen when informal arrangements were completed and had met Alphonsus on several occasions, could offer no serious objections to her parents' wishes for a marriage.[17]

A major part of the attraction of the arrangement for Don Joseph was Donna Teresa's status as an only child and the certainty that she would eventually inherit a very large estate. Yielding to the wishes of her father, Don Francis, Don Joseph agreed to postpone formal betrothal of the couple for a year or two to allow Alphonsus to become more firmly established in his career.

In the interval, however, events took an unexpected turn. The Princess of Presiccio, childless since the birth of Teresa, now gave birth to a son and heir, thus completely upsetting Don Joseph's hopes of financial gain. While not actually turning his back on the family, Don Joseph managed to make his visits gradually less frequent and his conversations rapidly turned to other matters. He hoped the matter would be forgotten gracefully; but it was not. His manipulations roused the smoldering resentment of young Teresa as well as that of her parents.

The young heir's life was brief, and soon Teresa was once again a potential heiress. In spite of a genuine affection for Alphonsus, she violently opposed Don Joseph's clumsy attempts to renew plans for a marriage between the two families.[18]

The time for resolving the conflict between his father's ambition and his own desires for service gradually drew nearer for Alphonsus. Responding to the invitation of a longtime friend, Francis Capecelatro, Duke of Carbona, he attended a Lenten retreat in 1722 conducted by a Vincentian priest, Father Vincent Cutica.[19] Judging from the later comments of Alphonsus himself, the retreat offered him the opportunity to solidify the doubts about his way of life and to ask himself openly: "What is the Spirit asking of me?"

By the end of the retreat he had come to at least a partial decision; he would resist the efforts of his father to arrange *any* marriage for him. Later he was to write to the Vincentian Fathers: "It was during a retreat in your house that I learned to know God...."[20]

During another retreat made six months afterwards, his resolution became even more definite: he would take a private vow of celibacy and surrender his rights as heir of the Liguori estates to his brother, Hercules. Later he spoke of this period as "the time of my conversion." Alphonsus, though, still had a long road to travel in his search for the spirit within his own heart.

Each day he would seek out a church in Naples and spend an hour kneeling in the Eucharistic presence of Jesus. Throughout his life, his prayer always began and ended somehow in the Eucharistic mystery of God's love for all men.

Although he had resolved never to marry, Alphonsus had not actually informed his father of his decision. Knowing the efforts of Don Joseph on his behalf, he sensed that the time when he could no longer remain silent was approaching. A second tentative matrimonial arrangement was negotiated by Don Joseph between Alphonsus and the daughter of the Duke of Prezenzano. Rather than openly reveal his decision to his father, Alphonsus chose to outwardly follow his wishes, hoping that God would once more intervene to prevent the marriage. When Don Joseph discoursed at great length on the beauty, talent, and high rank of his choice, Alphonsus only countered with reminders about his own sometimes weak health.

Halfheartedly, he appeared at a succession of dinner parties and receptions designed to bring the two young people together, but he gave the young lady no reason to hope for a future affectionate response. Finally, frustrated by the young man's apparent indifference, she demanded that her parents break the engagement. Don Joseph was crushed for the second time.

At this point Alphonsus sought an ally in his mother. Revealing to her his resolution to live a life of celibacy, he begged her to help win Don Joseph's consent.

Alphonsus was, in fact, wrestling with a more immediate problem which weighed far heavier on his mind. Throughout this period of his manhood he was suffering from wave after wave of scruples that his director, Father Pagano seemed unable to abate. Alphonsus was proud of his talent, but pride seemed a sin. He enjoyed the praise of others, but was this, too, wrong? His future held nothing but promise, but was this, too, somehow wrong? His vision of God, at this point, was one inherited from his Neopolitan background in history. God was often a punishing father, and his own image of father was reinforcing in this respect.

At this crisis point, Alphonsus was offered a case that was already the talk of Naples. Both the Grand Duke of Tuscany and a leading Neopolitan nobleman claimed ownership of an estate valued at 600,000[21] ducats (about half a million dollars). Lawyers of the best reputation and ability were engaged by both sides, and Alphonsus was entrusted with pleading a case that was a prize among his colleagues.

Confident of his ability to present the case favorably, Alphonsus prepared carefully for the court date. He appeared before the tribunal convinced that his client held legal right to the property and ready for the greatest victory of his career.

His former teacher, Dominic Caravita, dean of the best judges in Naples, presided, and an overcrowded courtroom listened attentively, if somewhat noisily, to the arguments of both sides. The case seemed comparatively clear-cut, turning on the simple question of feudal rights. Colleagues applauded the simplicity and logic of Alphonsus' argument.

His opponent listened carefully to Alphonsus' presentation, impressed with his confidence and calculated delivery. When Alphonsus had finally finished, however, he slowly drew himself to a standing position and, instead of proceeding with his own argument, stated simply: "You have wasted your breath. You have overlooked a document that destroys your whole case."[22] His opponent quickly produced the same piece of paper that Alphonsus had already read and reread in preparing the case. Suddenly Alphonsus noticed a small clause to which he had previously attached no importance, upon which all arguments in the case rested. The title was governed by either Lombardian or Angevin law, and this clearly decided the case in favor of his opponent.[23] Alphonsus' confidence visibly crumbled; he had lost his case because he had not sifted the evidence carefully enough. Immediately he conceded the case to his opponent. The gallery thundered.

Those who knew Alphonsus never questioned the sincerity of his mistake. But there were those who wondered if he had, perhaps, deliberately concealed the damning piece of evidence in the hope of gaining victory. Alphonsus felt that his own carelessness had caused a client financial loss of vast proportion, a loss he could never hope to repay.[24] Stunned, the young lawyer left the courtroom and found his way home, locking himself in his room. Alphonsus would never again return to the courtroom.

What prompted him to turn his back on his legal career? Was he simply unable to face the consequences of his own mistake? This judgment does not seem in keeping with his character. Throughout his life, he was willing to face his limitations. Was he a coward? It does not seem so. How much easier it would have been to listen to friends, including President Caravita himself, who reminded him that more experienced lawyers than he had made greater mistakes and survived. Or did he see in the situation one more proof that his heart did not really belong in this work?

Wrestling with the warring forces within himself, Alphonsus refused to leave his room. When his mother called him to dinner, he did not appear. The following day, fearing what would happen when Don Joseph returned to the house, his mother begged her son to leave his room and eat something.

On the third day his father, already having learned of the incident at court, returned home. No amount of persuasion or threat of force could dislodge his son from the locked room. In anguish, Donna Anna moaned: "He will die of hunger." Angered at his own inability to rouse his son, Don Joseph retorted: "Well, let him."[25]

Finally, four days after the onset of the crisis, Alphonsus responded to his mother's pleading, and opened the door. The sight of her son, gaunt and miserable in the midst of the greatest storm of his youth, moved Anna to tears.

During this time of solitude, more forcefully than ever, a single question plagued Alphonsus: "Lord, what do you want of me?" God had not provided an answer, but Alphonsus knew that his future did not rest in the profession of law. Abandoning his practice and turning his former clients over to friends, he withdrew again to the silence of his room. Rarely emerging except to seek the Eucharistic presence of Jesus, he devoted himself to a program of prayer. Instead of searching out the company of former friends, he visited more and more the patients at the Hospital of the Incurables. Tormented by scruples, he sought the direction of his lifelong friend, Father Pagano, and followed his advice without question. "Doubts and inquietudes," he tells us later, "often kept me in anguish: but my blind obedience to Father Pagano helped to calm those interior storms."[26]

Don Joseph interpreted his son's voluntary withdrawal as a temporary reaction to his crushing disappointment in court. But as time went on and Alphonsus did not resume his former way of life, a confrontation between the two became inevitable. Don Joseph approached Alphonsus with a legal matter that involved the Liguori family, and asked him to take care of it for him. "Father," Alphonsus painfully replied, "I beg you to ask someone else. I have spent my last day in Court."[27] The powerful Captain of the Galleys stared at his son, unable to accept what he had heard. In one stroke Alphonsus had toppled every hope Don Joseph had for his future. Plans he had made since the day of Alphonsus' birth were now never to be fulfilled.

Alphonsus' conscience was in a state of violent turmoil. "If I resist my father's authority, I am doing wrong," he reasoned. "But if I follow my father's wishes, when it does not seem to be God's will, won't I be doing worse?"

With his questions about the future still unanswered, he headed toward the Hospital of the Incurables. While serving the patients, a single thought echoed and reechoed through his mind: "Give yourself to me." Shocked at the depth and clarity of the experience, he found it difficult to regain his composure long enough to finish making the bed he had begun. Later, as he descended the stairs, the whole building seemed to vibrate beneath his feet, and again, in the depths of his consciousness, a voice seemed to repeat: "Give yourself to me." Shaking, he responded: "Lord, what do you will that I do?"[28]

Instead of returning to the Liguori palace, Alphonsus turned his steps toward the church of Our Lady of Ransom where a novena preceding the feast of the Assumption was in progress. Presenting himself at the feet of Our Lady, he begged her for the grace to know God's will and the strength to carry it out. Here, for the third time, the sensation that had overcome him at the hospital welled up in his heart. He had already offered to surrender to God's will, but what *was* that will?

Surrendering to the impulse of the Spirit, Alphonsus consecrated himself to the service of God and resolved to seek the priesthood. Further, he pledged to enter the Congregation of the Oratory as soon as possible. As a symbol of his dedication, he slowly unbuckled his sword, the mark of his nobility, and laid it carefully at the feet of Our Lady of Ransom.[29]

Leaving the church, Alphonsus turned in the direction of the Oratory to reveal to Father Pagano the happenings of this decisive day, but his director's reply caught him off guard. "Such things are not decided in a moment," he said. "I will let you know what I think of it in a year." "A year?" Alphonsus demanded. "I don't want to wait even a day." "My son," Pagano replied, "you must allow your resolutions to mature and pray very hard to know the true will of God for you."[30]

When he returned to the palace, Alphonsus resolved to begin a three-day fast. Throwing himself into a life of even deeper prayer, he at last found the peace he had sought for so long.

When Alphonsus again told Father Pagano of his ardent desire for the priesthood, Father Pagano acknowledged that the call seemed to be from God; but counseled him that as his director he would not permit him to join the Oratory without his father's consent, and that seemed an impossibility.

Unaware of his son's resolution, Don Joseph returned from the country villa at Marianella and lost no time pleading with Alphonsus not to destroy his hopes for him. One day, in a fit of frustrated grief, he turned to his son and sputtered: "I pray to God to take one of us out of this world; I cannot stand the sight of you." The response of Alphonsus was not the one Don Joseph expected. He calmly replied: "God is my only refuge, since my own father abandons me."[31]

Alphonsus saw now the futility of concealing his decision, and stated openly: "I have made an irrevocable resolution to enter the Oratory and to consecrate myself to God. Please do not be angry. I ask your blessing."[32] Don Joseph left the room, leaving behind him a trail of insults.

The announcement had greater consequences for the head of the Liguori house than might first seem apparent. Two sons, Benedict and Cajetan, had already entered the priesthood. Hercules, the only remaining son, was only eighteen and might not live to produce a male heir. Alphonsus seemed the only hope of the house. Don Joseph became more convinced than ever that it was his duty to restore his son to his senses. At first he refused to speak to Alphonsus. Torn between loyalty to her husband and compassion for her son, Donna Anna pleaded with both parties to end their cold war. Neither would yield.

Sensing the futility of open hostility, the Captain sent for Alphonsus and explained to him, in tones of kindness and concern, the many reasons he should obey his father's wishes. Embracing him as only an Italian father can, he begged his son to pity his aging father. Alphonsus wept, but, again, he did not yield.

As a last resort, Don Joseph turned to friends he knew Alphonsus respected. Muzio di Maio, President of the Royal Court, pleaded with him on his father's behalf, but Alphonsus replied: "I must follow the will of God."[33] Father de Miro, Benedictine abbot, stressed the respect and honor he owed his father. Alphonsus responded: "Your view of the matter is not mine. I am certain that God is calling me; I must be faithful to that call."[34]

Alphonsus did not battle his father completely without support. Father Pagano, his director, and Father Vincent Cutica, the Vincentian who had conducted the retreat a few months earlier that had begun his long journey to this point, supported him before Don Joseph.[35]

In desperation, the Captain turned to his brother-in-law,

Monsignor Cavalieri, Bishop of Troia, who was visiting in Naples. Instead of agreeing with Don Joseph, however, the aging bishop heartily replied: "I myself surrendered my rights as eldest son in order to become a priest, and you expect me to tell your son to do the opposite?" Monsignor Cavalieri begged his brother-in-law to withdraw opposition to the resolution of Alphonsus, assuring him that he too was convinced that the call came from God.[36]

At last, Don Joseph surrendered. Granting his permission for Alphonsus to seek the priesthood, he insisted, however, that he renounce any thought of entering the Oratory. Following the advice of Father Pagano, Alphonsus accepted this condition of his father.

On October 23, 1723, at the age of twenty-seven, Alphonsus exchanged the clothing of a Neopolitan nobleman for that of a young seminarian.[37] One year had passed since he had first resolved to seek the will of God.

CHAPTER 2

Mission to the Poorest

Alphonsus began his clerical studies, as he had his legal preparation, under his father's roof. This was not unusual, since many Neopolitan young men training for the priesthood chose to follow a similar course; and arch-episcopal decrees provided a framework of regulations and a detailed course of study that was to be followed by candidates for ordination who chose to be educated by private tutors attached to the seminary, rather than follow a normal course of study.[1]

The study of canon law already behind him, Alphonsus turned to an intensive study of dogmatic and moral theology. Throughout his preparation, the young man found himself returning again and again to three sources that were to form the bedrock of his life and teaching: the gospel, the works of Saint Thomas Aquinas, and the works of Saint Teresa of Avila. The gospel became his daily companion and the source of a new and deeper understanding of Jesus the Redeemer.[2] He made a special study of the doctrine of Saint Thomas, and again and again throughout his life he would turn to the logic and insight of this great Doctor of the Church. The writings of Saint Teresa of Avila led him to a deeper understanding of the Christian life, helping him to see the connection between theoretical doctrine and the realities of daily existence. As his special patroness and guide, she led him back to the source he had already found central: the person of Jesus.[3] The familiar salutation at the beginning of letters he penned himself, "Live Jesus, Mary, Joseph and Teresa," witnesses to his lifelong devotion to this extraordinary spiritual guide.

The former nobleman, Alphonsus Liguori, reverently served Mass each morning in the parish church of San Angelo. Working as a humble catechist, he gathered the children of the parish from street corners and led them to the church. Simply, gently, he spoke to them of Jesus and prepared them for their first Holy Communion. The lawyer who had held spectators spellbound in the courtroom less than a year before now searched for images and examples to help draw children to a deeper love of God.

Many of his former acquaintances shut their doors to the shabby young cleric. Even Don Joseph later admitted that he would cross to the opposite side of the street before he would confront his son in public.[4] Abandoned by many of those he considered friends, Alphonsus found peace in the Eucharistic presence of Jesus.

One day while occupying his usual place during solemn exposition of the Eucharist, he attracted the renewed curiosity of three other students for the priesthood. John Mazzini, Joseph Panza, and Joseph Porpora had previously been drawn by the apparent devotion of a young nobleman; now they observed a cleric occupying the same place and bearing a striking resemblance to this person. Finally, they resolved to make the acquaintance of this young man and waited until he left the church. After ascertaining that he was, indeed, the same person, they could not resist asking: "How did such a change take place?" Alphonsus answered simply: "It was God's will."[5] Walking slowly down the stairs and across the piazza, the four began to speak of their mutual dreams and desires, and promised to help each other grow in the love of God. Their friendship was to play an important part in the destiny of Alphonsus.

December 23, 1724, Alphonsus received minor orders.[6] Hoping to serve as a missionary either in the kingdom of Naples or in China, he applied for admission to the Society of the Propaganda.[7] The following June he served as catechist for an extensive mission conducted by the famous Canon Gizzio, one of the directors of the Society, on the small island of Procida off the coast of Naples.

His zeal enkindled, he soon applied for admission to the ranks of the White Fathers, an association of diocesan clergy founded in

Naples by Saint James della Marca in 1430. The apostolate of the society was to comfort prisoners condemned to death. Even after his ordination, Alphonsus devoted a portion of his time to this important work. He tried to speak to those he befriended in a language they would understand, making use of images and examples geared to their experience. "God loves you," he would tell them. "Believe in him; return to him. He will save you as he saved the good thief who shared his death, and he will bring you to the joy of everlasting life."[8] Many years later Alphonsus would write a short treatise based on his own early work with condemned prisoners. Many examples contained in a later work, *Preparation for Death*,[9] were also intended to serve this purpose.

On April 6, 1726, Alphonsus was raised to the diaconate and the archbishop granted him permission to preach in all the churches of Naples. His first sermon delivered during Forty Hours devotion in the church of Saint John dealt with the love of Jesus expressed in the Holy Eucharist. The response to his approach was so great that many pastors invited him to preach the same devotion in their own parishes.

Only months before his ordination, Alphonsus collapsed. Already weakened by arduous study, the schedule of constant preaching had undermined his damaged health. Several doctors examined him and offered little hope. Don Joseph and Donna Anna witnessed the last sacraments being administered to their son with heavy hearts.

Alphonsus requested that a statue of Our Lady of Ransom be brought to him. Four years earlier he had laid his sword at her feet as a symbol of his "conversion"; now he desired to renew his act of surrender to the will of her Son. As he sought to unite himself anew with the ultimate will of God, the crisis passed.

After a period of three months spent in quiet convalescence, Alphonsus began a retreat of ten days in preparation for his ordination. On Saturday, December 2, 1726, he was ordained priest of God by Bishop Dominic Inviti.[10] The following morning his parents saw their son celebrate Mass for the first time. The following prayer which he composed early in his priestly life, might well have been on his lips as he ascended the altar steps:

O my Lord, I am about to offer your blood for sin-
ners, and for myself, the most ungrateful of all. I offer it
to obtain from your mercy the grace to always remain
worthy to celebrate Holy Mass. I not only ask to perse-
vere in grace but also to grow ever in your love, so that I
might always choose your will before my own.[11]

From the beginning of his priestly career, Alphonsus was attracted to the ideal of a life of active contemplation. Using as his
model the life of Jesus the Redeemer, he committed himself to
intense prayer and penance from which flowed the strength to
touch others with the love of God.

Once a month, with the three young priests he had met at the
Forty Hours devotion, and his friend, Januarius Sarnelli, son of
the Baron of Ciorani, Alphonsus traveled to the country house of
Michael de Alteriis for a day of special prayer. Each found new
strength in their day together, and drew from common prayer
new strength for their daily apostolate. Alphonsus shared with
them his concern for the poor.

Listening to the baroque style of preaching in vogue during
the period, and watching the uncomprehending faces of those in the
congregations, Alphonsus resolved to speak in ordinary terms to
ordinary people.[12] His experience teaching children and serving condemned convicts had changed the style of the once-famous lawyer.

Alphonsus spoke simply and turned to examples familiar to
his listeners to illustrate each point. Paradoxically, the sermons he
prepared with the simplest "lazzaroni" in mind were soon attended
by lawyers, noblemen, government officials, and other priests.

The story is told of the time Nicholas Capasso, the famous
Neopolitan satirist, confronted Alphonsus outside the church after
listening to one of his sermons. "Don Nicholas," the young priest
said, "I see you always in the congregation; are you preparing a
satire on my style?" "Of course not," Capasso answered. "I listen
to you because you forget yourself and preach Jesus Christ."[13]

In the confessional Alphonsus departed sharply from the
rigorists and pessimists whose influence dominated so much of
the spiritual life of the kingdom of Naples and his own early religious training. "The more deeply a soul is enslaved," he used to

say, "the more necessary it becomes to use gentleness to free it from its chains."[14] The young priest spoke simply of Christ and stressed God's mercy instead of God's wrath. Because of this, demands on his time became unmanageable.

On steaming summer evenings Alphonsus would gather those who wished to come—lazzaroni, workers, fishermen—and would speak of God's love for them. Other young priests helped in the effort, and soon crowds gathered around the zealous preachers.

Twisted rumors soon reached the archbishop of secret meetings by those planning to overthrow the Church and the State by agitating crowds of the poor. The archbishop reported the rumors to the governor who sent an undercover agent to attend the next meeting. Standing at the edge of a large crowd, he could barely hear what the leaders were saying, but he became suspicious of the wrapt attention they seemed to be commanding, and recommended to his superiors that the ringleaders be arrested when the next gathering took place.[15]

Alphonsus happened to be visiting the archbishop when news of the pending arrests arrived. Realizing that the orders referred to himself and his companions, he hastened to call off the meeting. But the cardinal, fearing that further rumors would damage the reputation of the rising young preacher, commanded him to discontinue the gatherings.

Alphonsus knew that the Church must not always wait for people to come to her doors, but she must also be prepared to go to the people. But in obedience to the archbishop, he discontinued active leadership of the group. Two converts, Barbarese, a school master, and Nardonne, a former army deserter, carried on the work, drawing on Alphonsus for advice.[16] To avoid further governmental interference, it was suggested that they discontinue the routine of meeting on street corners and find some sort of arrangement indoors. At first they met in a barber shop; later they transferred meetings to a chapel belonging to the hatmakers guild.[17]

Soon there were many converts to the movement and centers throughout the city. The group later became known as the Association of Chapels. Alphonsus delivered conferences whenever he could and continued to encourage the group. As membership grew, the chapels were placed under the direction of parish priests and were approved by the archdiocese and acceptable confraternities. By 1500 Naples claimed sixty-five chapels and members numbering thirty thousand.[18]

As a member of the Propaganda, Alphonsus was also pledged to preach a number of missions outside Naples. In Bari and Campagna and Bosco, Alphonsus labored with his companions to respond to the needs of the country people, to bring them back to the God he knew loved them so much.

As his commitments became more numerous and his life of prayer more intense, Alphonsus became more restless. He could no longer remain under his father's roof; he could not practice the complete poverty he longed to embrace within the walls of the Liguori palace.

An opportunity soon presented itself in the form of a request from Father Matthew Ripa that Alphonsus accept the chaplaincy of the new College of the Holy Family in Naples. Known as "the Chinese College,"[19] it was founded to help educate native Chinese clergy for the missions. Bringing with him five young converts, Matthew Ripa had returned from twenty years in China with great hopes for the future.[20]

Seeing in the offer an opportunity to become more closely involved in missionary activity, and also appreciating the freedom of movement that the post would permit him, Alphonsus, after consulting Father Pagano, willingly accepted. The struggling young community offered Alphonsus many chances to increase his poverty of spirit. Often, the meal he joyously shared consisted of radish soup and a piece of fruit.

Doubling his acts of mortification, the young priest became accustomed to studying while standing or pacing back and forth in his small cell. His bed became a narrow board or the bare floor, as he struggled to imitate the Redeemer who "had no place to lay his head." And yet, in spite of all his efforts to open himself completely to the will of God, Alphonsus underwent constant psychological stress. The peace and joy he had formerly experienced in prayer disappeared. Plunged into darkness, the young priest cried out: "I go to Jesus and he refuses me. I turn to Mary and she hears me not."[21] Turning to his director as his only hope of knowing the will of God, he followed Father Pagano's instructions to the letter and continued to pray even when he had to force himself to his knees.

In spite of the personal conflict that churned within him, Alphonsus assumed his duties in the chapel with all the energy that he possessed. When crowds overflowed the chapel to listen to him on Sunday, he scheduled other services during the week. Often he spoke of Mary, the Mother of all Christians, of the love of Jesus expressed in the gift of the Holy Eucharist, and of the confidence we must have in the promises of Christ.

When he was not before the altar or in the pulpit, Alphonsus could often be found in the confessional, remaining there even far into the night if the numbers who wished to receive the sacrament necessitated it. Paradoxically, he never experienced in himself the same light that his direction brought to other souls. And yet, because of his own interior trials, he knew instinctively how to calm and encourage those who came to him.[22]

Resolving never to waste a moment of time, Alphonsus continued the support of the Association of Chapels and when members of the Propaganda requested it, he conducted missions. While preaching a mission in Marano, his appearance drew the attention of several people. One of them remarked: "If his sermons are anything like his cassock, we are all in a bad way."[23]

After preaching three missions in rapid succession, at Capodimonte, Casoria, and the parish of Annunziata in Naples, Alphonsus was once again on the point of collapse. Realizing how close he really was to exhaustion, Alphonsus agreed to spend a few weeks away from his regular duties. With five friends (Mazzini, Mannarini, Panza, Porpora, and Joris), he set out for the Amalfi coast. A few hours out, a violent storm washed them back to the coast of Minori, and they settled down to wait for a break in the weather.

At the home of the archbishop, they met the vicar general of Scala, who urged them to spend a holiday at Santa Maria dei Monti, near Scala.[24] He told them of an abandoned house with a nearby chapel where they could reserve the Blessed Sacrament, and also granted them faculties in case they might wish to work with the shepherds of the area. Such an invitation they could hardly refuse, so the six priests gratefully set out for Maria dei Monti.

CHAPTER 3

Seeds of Scala

Four miles from the town of Scala they reached their journey's end. The view that greeted their eyes as they completed their climb was staggering. Mountains still towered over them. On one side their eyes traveled along miles of green coastline dotted with tiny clusters of houses clinging high above the sea. Below them, and as far as the distant horizon, stretched the sparkling blue waters of the Mediterranean. On the other side the Appenines stretched like fingers to the sky. If peace could be found in nature anywhere on earth, it could be found in this place.

No sooner had they unpacked their meager belongings and placed the Blessed Sacrament in the tabernacle of the tiny chapel, when they discovered that they were no longer alone. A few scattered peasants and goatherds had heard of the arrival of the priests and had come to see them.

Alphonsus and the others spoke to them kindly, questioning them about their needs. His career had not prepared him for the spiritual starvation of the mountain people who came to his doorstep all that day.[1] All of his priestly life had been spent among those who lived in the large cities of the kingdom of Naples, where there was a need for someone to take a special interest in the poor.

Although Alphonsus labored among the people considered the most abandoned—prisoners, prostitutes, children of the streets, those dying of wretched diseases—he sensed they were in one sense rich. These poor shepherds had no priest at all, no catechist, no one who cared for their needs. Most of them barely remembered that God existed, and certainly they were not convinced that he cared about them and their life on a lonely mountain.

The missionaries set to work with the fervor that matched the needs of the people who were crowding around them. They offered Mass, instructed the people, and prepared those who were able to receive the sacraments. Shepherds who received the Word traveled to other areas nearby, and soon new arrivals found their way to the door of the unintentional missionaries. No one was turned away. The vacation turned into one of the longest missions Alphonsus was ever to conduct.

News of the work of the missionaries reached the bishop of Scala, and he pleaded with the group to return again to his diocese. Alphonsus finally agreed to return the following month to preach the novena of the Holy Cross at the cathedral, and left for Naples a changed man. He had gone to Scala seeking refuge from a storm and had found a need so great that he was compelled to find a way to fill it.

Returning to Naples, Alphonsus encountered Father Thomas Falcoia, who was preparing to leave for Rome, where he would be consecrated bishop of Castellamare. During his stay at the Chinese College Alphonsus had come to know Father Falcoia very well. The story of the humiliation Father Falcoia had suffered as a result of events at Scala had been common knowledge at Naples.[2]

While preaching a mission in Scala eleven years before, in 1719, Father Falcoia had received a request to reorganize a contemplative community that was on the brink of collapse. With the blessing and financial assistance of his superior, Father Filangieri of the Pious Workers,[3] he undertook the work.

On May 20, 1720, twelve postulants in this contemplative community began their religious life under the direction of Father Falcoia. Intending to give this group the rule of the Visitation, he requested that a professed Visitation nun from Naples assume responsibility for forming the sisters according to the Visitation rule. The request was denied.[4] Yet, despite this obstacle, the number of members grew to thirty in less than three years.

In 1724, a twenty-seven-year-old postulant was admitted: Maria Celeste Crostarosa. The previous eight years of her life had been spent under the Carmelite rule, but her convent had been dissolved.[5] Falcoia had given a retreat at the convent, and when he learned of their difficulty, he offered to extend refuge to Maria Celeste and two of her companions.

Sister Maria Celeste records in her autobiography the following version of what happened when she had been a novice for less than six months.

> On Rogation Monday in the year 1725, after receiving Holy Communion as usual, I experienced within a brief space of time an intimate transformation of my soul in Jesus Christ Our Lord. I felt as though I had exchanged the present life for the unspeakable joys of eternity. In that moment I received an outpouring of the most precious blessings contained in the life of Our Saviour. Jesus told me that He wished to use me to establish in the world a new Institute, of which all the rules should have reference to the imitation of His divine example. The impression left on me was so deep that it could never be effaced from my memory.[6]

Sister Maria Celeste also insisted that on the feast of Corpus Christi Our Lord revealed to her the rule and habit that were to be adopted by members of the new Institute, and ordered her to make his wishes known to her director. The same experience was reported by Sister Mary Columba and other religious.[7]

Since Father Falcoia was in Rome at the time, Sister Maria Celeste confided her experience to her novice mistress, Sister Maria Angela. After listening carefully to the details related by the young novice, the mistress directed her to put the details in writing, send it to Father Falcoia, and remain otherwise silent about the affair until further directed.

Arriving at Naples from Rome, Falcoia opened the letter from Maria Celeste describing her experience in detail. Fearing that the "vision" might be the product of her own imagination, he answered that only someone filled with pride would believe such nonsense, and he commanded her to throw the rule she claimed was the result of the vision into the fire.

Somehow, the letter from Father Falcoia dated June 30 did

not arrive at the convent until after the feast of the Assumption.[8] The rule that Falcoia had commanded Maria Celeste to burn had already arrived at Naples. As he read the various items of the rule carefully, Falcoia was amazed to recognize in it something that he himself had experienced many years before.

One day while walking along the Tiber with a friend, Falcoia experienced an intense interior conviction that God willed the foundation of a new religious Institute of both men and women whose goal would be to imitate as closely as possible the virtues of the Redeemer.[9]

He had tried several times to make his vision a reality. In 1710, he left Rome for Naples where he tried for four years to convince others to share the work. Every attempt ended in failure.[10] Plans for the work had to be shelved when, in 1714, he was elected general superior of the Pious Workers. While willingly fulfilling the duties of his office, he could not remove the idea completely from his mind.

When his term of office ended he again took up plans for forming the new community. While conducting a mission at Tarentum, he finally found twelve priests who agreed to live a community life based on a rule that bound them to imitate Christ the Redeemer in all things, and to preach the gospel to the poor. This attempt also ended in failure.[11]

Once again God seemed to be reinforcing his will through the instrumentality of the novice, Maria Celeste, for the rule that was now before him centered on that same idea. Perhaps, he thought, this was the real reason that the Visitation nuns had refused to help them implement an existing rule!

In spite of his own conviction that the spirit of God was guiding the advent of a new Institute, Falcoia presented the rule to several theologians for their opinions. Every one of them stated that there seemed to be no objection to implementing it, since the community at Scala had no existing rule. Only the consent of the professed religious stood in the path of making the rule a reality.

Convening a chapter, Falcoia asked them to accept or reject the proposed rule. With the exception of the superioress and two professed religious, the religious voted to accept it. The superioress insisted that more time was needed before such a serious change could be carried out. She asked to be allowed to consult Father

Filangieri of the Pious Workers who, as Father Falcoia's superior, had first asked him to direct the Scala community.

After listening to Maria Celeste's version of the events surrounding the presentation of the rule, Father Filangieri opposed the entire undertaking. He published a directive stating that (1) the vision at Scala was the work of the devil, (2) that Maria Celeste was the victim of hallucination, and (3) that Father Falcoia was not responsible for his actions.[12] News of the declaration spread the length of Naples almost as soon as it was written.

History might question the validity of such a declaration, even if it cannot know the motives that prompted it. Filangieri had no real part in the work, nor had he interviewed any of the people directly involved in the matter. But once the declaration was made public, the damage was done.

Further, Filangieri attempted to persuade the sisters to drive Maria Celeste from the convent; they refused. And as a last precaution, he forbade Falcoia to set foot within the convent or even to correspond with the members.

The following letter addressed to the convent reflects the spirit in which Falcoia accepted the humiliation.

I see now how much God loves you. He it is who is removing every obstacle to your perfection, and His hand will restore the order which has been disturbed, not through your fault, but by my lack of skill. The Father General, I would have you know, has treated me as I deserve in accusing me of folly and delusion. Submit then in peace to the prohibition he has imposed on me against taking part in the affairs of the convent. Live ever in obedience, and pray to the Divine Master for us. For my part I will never cease to pray for my most dear daughters, to whom I give a last blessing from the bottom of my heart.[13]

For a few years, Falcoia had no direct contact with the sisters of Scala. But now, as he spoke to Alphonsus, he was free of many of the bonds that prevented him from renewing contact with the tiny community. He had been raised to the see of Castellamare which was very close to Scala. The superior of the convent was now

Sister Maria Angela, who had filled the post of mistress of novices at the time of the vision of Maria Celeste. And finally, a stroke had removed Filangieri from the picture.[14] Alphonsus listened carefully to Falcoia's explanation of events at Scala. He sympathized with his efforts while remaining skeptical about the validity of Maria Celeste's vision. But he agreed to conduct a retreat at the convent when he returned to Scala to preach the novena of the Holy Cross. Such an arrangement would help him to judge the situation for himself. But neither Falcoia nor Alphonsus realized the role the former lawyer was about to play in shaping the destiny of the new Institute.

In September 1730, Alphonsus traveled to Scala with two companions. Falcoia had already written to Sister Maria Angela, instructing her to receive Alphonsus and to follow his direction as they would his own.

After preaching the novena of the Holy Cross, Alphonsus went directly to the convent. Knowing that nothing could be accomplished until the matter of the rule was settled once and for all, he instructed Sister Maria Angela to describe as accurately as she could all that had taken place.

The following day Alphonsus interviewed each sister separately, beginning with Sister Maria Celeste. Her brief account follows:

> Don Alphonsus began by commanding me to relate the whole story of my life, and all the graces which God had given me from my childhood....Then I came to the divine communication concerning the new Rule and the new Institute, and I concealed nothing from him of the fears which had assailed me, or of the persecution of which I was made the victim. The next witnesses were Mary Columba and some of the others more or less favored with the same light. After them, all of the sisters, including the former superioress, had to give their opinions.[15]

Alphonsus weighed the evidence before him and sought the light to know the will of God in prayer. Then he gathered the community and revealed his decision. He was certain, he said, that God was the author of this work, and that those who had branded it a hallucination were mistaken. He encouraged the religious to thank God for the grace that he had given them, and suggested that they adopt the rule as soon as possible. Aware that a few of the sisters had openly opposed such a step, Alphonsus was careful to remind them of the grave responsibility that was involved in opposing the will of God.

The former superioress, who had created such a chaos a few years before, slowly rose and faced the community, declaring slowly and deliberately: "If such is the will of God, then I not only give up my opposition, but declare myself the first to accept the new rule."[16]

The community was ready to embrace the new rule but the authorization of Bishop Guerriero, bishop of Scala had to be secured before they could obtain their long-desired goal. The situation was a difficult one. Two previous upheavals at the convent involving Falcoia had not been forgotten in the diocese; and now that he had assumed jurisdiction at Castellamare, there was the added possibility that any action on the part of the newly appointed bishop might seem like "digging in someone else's backyard." The safest course for the bishop of Scala to pursue might well be to let matters remain as they were.

Weighing the alternatives, Alphonsus decided to present the case to the bishop himself before returning to Naples. Carefully outlining the facts as he understood them, he told the bishop that, in his judgment, the convent should be granted authorization to adopt the rule. The bishop respected the judgment of the young priest. Placing the matter completely in his hands, he authorized Alphonsus to organize the convent according to the new rule. Alphonsus returned to the sisters and suggested to them that the rule be formally adopted on the feast of Pentecost of the following spring (1731).

Finally, Father Liguori began the retreat that he had originally come to conduct. He chose as his theme the person of Jesus, the Redeemer. As he developed his theme he poured into it the fruits of his own prayer and study of the gospels. By the end of the retreat, Alphonsus considered each of the sisters a "daughter in Christ," and they in turn called him "father."

Returning to Naples, Alphonsus soon received a letter from Falcoia who had heard of the effect of his teaching.

> My daughters consider the retreat you have given them as a great grace. They were good before. Thanks to you, I shall find them better. In their name and my own I thank you with all my heart: you whom I venture to call my son, since you were so good as to give me the affectionate name of "father."[17]

At the same time, letters from the sisters at the convent asking for advice and counsel began to arrive. The answer offered by Alphonsus to his new spiritual daughters is certainly one of the most personal and beautiful among the thousands that have been preserved. The warmth of his concern and his friendship fills every paragraph.

> Naples
> Oct. 29, 1730
>
> May Jesus and Mary always possess our hearts! Finish your work, O Lord, and take complete possession of our hearts.
>
> I received your first letters on the feast of my patroness, Saint Teresa. It was a consolation for me only to see the envelope, for it told me who had written those letters....
>
> I wish to tell you that though some time has elapsed since my stay at Scala (less than a month), my remembrance of you is as vivid as if I had departed only yesterday....
>
> Courage, then, my Sisters, do not grow careless in praying for me. I, who am a priest called to save souls, should be filled with zeal for the glory of God. You must know that the very thought that you are praying for me gives me courage, and spurs me on to give pleasure to God, as it seems to me almost impossible that God can refuse to hear you when you pray earnestly for some soul, and say to him as Saint Teresa used to say: "Lord we wish to ob-

tain this for our friend." How discouraged I should feel if you should stop praying for me. It seems that I pray more for you than for myself; for myself, I try to be resigned if God wills me to remain in the last place; but as for you, I will not rest until I see you all like Seraphim.

From time to time I turn towards your home and think: "Love Jesus." Love him then, do not lose a moment of time. Remember that he loves you without ceasing; he loses no time. Speak to him often, especially when you find yourselves before him in the Blessed Sacrament; speak to him of love....[18]

After speaking to the community in such earnest terms, Alphonsus carefully jotted notes to each of the sisters who had written to him and signed himself: "Alfonso deLiguori, a wretched sinner."

But the same letter that reveals the heights of his desires also points up the depth of the conflict that still churned within his heart.

I am as well as can be expected during the storm. I am in such a state that at times I can see neither heaven nor hell, and I find myself within a dark abyss where no order, but everlasting horror dwells. (Job 10:22) May the will of God be ever done....O Lord, here I am, hell would be little for me.[19]

Alphonsus had endured such torment before; it would pursue him throughout his life. We fail to understand the dimensions of his character if we do not realize the struggle that demanded Alphonsus place such radical faith in his spiritual directors.

Exhaustion was soon added to the trials of the young missionary. He had in rapid succession preached a novena of the Holy Cross at Scala, worked to unravel the situation at the convent, conducted the sisters' annual retreat, returned to Naples only to begin a prolonged mission, and then departed for Amalfi to give even another retreat to a group of religious. Only four years had passed since his ordination and the critical illness that had preceded it.

In the middle of the retreat at Amalfi, Alphonsus was struck by an intense fever. After resting briefly, he managed to finish the retreat and return to Naples. Within a month he suffered a serious relapse. The fever returned; this time with such intensity that Matthew Ripa, head of the Chinese College, left business unfinished at Rome so that he might be at the bedside of his friend in his last moments. The fever settled in his lungs, inflicting lasting damage, and little hope seemed left.[20]

But for the second time in his life the crisis passed, and Alphonsus was forced into a period of convalescence that lasted for more than three months. This was a time to suffer and to think, to pray and to plan.

The feast of Pentecost was drawing closer (May 23, 1731), and the convent at Scala was experiencing a major storm. The focal point of the difficulty was once again Falcoia.

The revelation of Maria Celeste had presented only a sketchy outline of the rule that was to be adopted. If any sort of stability was to be achieved, a formal rule and constitutions had to be drafted in a form that would insure final approbation. Bishop Guerriero had agreed to approve the adoption only because of his confidence in the ability of Father Liguori, without considering the possible role of Falcoia.

Now Falcoia pleaded with Alphonsus.

> You obtained from the Bishop the reorganization of the convent, but now he means to carry it out after his own fashion. I beg you to use all your skill to bring him to terms. Let him allow me to settle the rule and steer this ship. I have directed this convent for many years, and I know all the difficulties which are no doubt in his mind. Besides, when I have drawn up the constitutions, I will submit them to him and be ready to modify anything of which he disapproves.[21]

The situation was a difficult one. Falcoia was asking Alphonsus to consult in matters that went far beyond his original agreement, and he knew it only too well. Alphonsus laid the matter before his confessor and immediate superior, Father Pagano, who advised him to avoid becoming involved in the situation; and Canon Torni positively ordered him to keep out of the discussion completely, under the circumstances.[22] Resigned to the will of God, he informed Falcoia of his decision.

The sisters of Scala were crushed. It seemed to them as though all their hopes and prayers would end in emptiness; for without the help of Alphonsus, success seemed impossible. Too many of Falcoia's opponents still agitated against him at Scala, and now he was further handicapped by his position as bishop of another diocese.

Only Maria Celeste seemed confident. Writing to Alphonsus she assured him:

> This prohibition against your concerning yourself with our affairs will not be persisted in; it is merely an exercise of your patience and ours. God did not send you to our convent without a particular plan. He did it for our future good, and not merely for the good you have already accomplished in the past. But God requires suffering. And those who are to help us must suffer with us. Since I heard of this prohibition I have not stopped praying. Our Lord has helped me realize that no one shall take from us the man whom he himself has given us for our support.[23]

Maria Celeste was right. Tempers cooled and Bishop Guerriero agreed to permit Falcoia to draw up the proposed constitutions, but only if Alphonsus would consent to revise and correct the work. Father Pagano agreed, and work on the new rule began. Within two years the work would be concluded, and Alphonsus would carefully revise and annotate each page. Falcoia then wrote Alphonsus.

> I rejoice in all this. The entire credit is due to you. Whatever reputation the convent now enjoys has come to it through you.[24]

Falcoia, working not only from the revelations granted to Maria Celeste but also from his own understanding of community life, prepared the letter of the rule. But it was Alphonsus who breathed into the letter of the rule a distinctive spirit. He translated the practice of the various virtues of the Redeemer into a unified vision of the Christian life, a life in closest union with the redemptive will of Jesus Christ and focused on the centrality of a life of prayer.

In spite of the peace his direction brought to the convent of San Salvatore at Scala, Alphonsus felt he was doing nothing for God. In the midst of one of his darkest hours, a letter arrived from a person he now considered a dear friend, Sister Maria Celeste.

> Father, I was asking God during the time of meditation, to grant that we should never be separated from Him, when I saw the throne of glory He is preparing for you in eternity in return for your love for Jesus and the work you are doing for his sake. "As a proof of my love for him," He told me, "*I will give to those he takes under his care an increase of grace and fervor.* Those who hear his words will draw from them an abundance of spiritual blessings. Tell him for me that I am pleased that he is working for the conversion of sinners, and especially that he is leading so many to a greater love of God." I tell you this, Father, because it is the will of God, to which I am bound to submit.[25]

The letter gave Alphonsus such consolation that he kept it until the end of his life, rereading it in other times of doubt and depression.

Autumn once again touched the slopes of Scala, and Alphonsus returned to preach the novena of the Holy Cross at the cathedral as he had the year before. As soon as he completed the novena, he began the annual retreat for the sisters of San Salvatore. He left the convent more firmly convinced than ever that each sister sincerely desired to become a woman of prayer, and that a spirit of Christian charity helped the community to respond as a single person to the will of God, even in difficult circumstances. He could not know that even before returning to Naples, an event would take place at the convent that would change the course of his life.

On October 3, 1731, Sister Maria Celeste experienced a second major apparition.

> It was evening, and we were about to enter the refectory. I was meditating on the holy patriarch of Assisi, whose feast was just beginning, when suddenly...I saw Our Lord with Saint Francis on his right hand and a halo of light about them both. On the left stood a priest whom Our Lord pointed out to me with his finger. It was Don Alphonsus de Liguori. Then Jesus said to me: "This is he whom I have chosen to be the head of my Institute, the Prefect General of a new Congregation of men who shall work for my glory." At the same time the Congregation itself appeared to me as already founded and in full action, whereupon I was filled with such joy that I was unable to take food that evening.[26]

Was the vision that Maria Celeste experienced from God? Or was it perhaps the fruit of her own imagination? Several facts weigh heavily on both sides. Was Celeste's imagination stirred by the recent presence of Alphonsus and his forceful description of the spirit of the rule? It was true, hers had been a life of prayer in every way. She had retained a spirit of obedience and union with the will of God despite persecution. Alphonsus himself considered Maria Celeste a saint. The dilemma would plague the minds and hearts of all connected with the convent for many years to come; a modern reader might be allowed to judge the facts as we now know them.

Sister Maria Celeste revealed her experience to Falcoia. Again, the bishop of Castellamare expressed a lack of faith in the visions, telling her:

> I put no faith in your revelations; and I suggest that you follow my example. Our conduct cannot be determined by your imagination. And if I ask you for the details of what you think you saw, my only reason is that such knowledge may help me to direct you.[27]

He further directed Maria Celeste not to reveal the vision to Alphonsus.

Almost contradicting his own stern written opinion, Falcoia immediately left for Scala to interview Maria Celeste personally. After listening to the details of the apparition, Falcoia concluded that the vision did express the will of God. It did, in fact, reinforce the intense manifestation that had lain fallow for twenty years in his own heart.

Writing to Alphonsus, the bishop told him of his plans to come to Naples soon to speak about a matter of great importance to him. Instead, Alphonsus journeyed to Castellamare.

In revealing the vision of Maria Celeste, Falcoia sought to persuade Alphonsus to make the dream a reality. Eagerly he pointed out the good that could be accomplished by the new congregation. Everything he said appealed to the desires of the young priest. Alphonsus longed to belong more closely to a community of priests who would not only try to reflect the redemptive qualities of Jesus but also dedicate themselves to the very mission of Christ, to preach the gospel to the poor.

Falcoia spoke of something he had realized so forcibly on his own first trip into the mountains near Scala. It seemed no one had bothered about the poor who wandered the hills of southern Italy, living a life of loneliness and poverty and living it without God.[28] In fact, one of the scandals of the Church in the kingdom of Naples was the large number of secular priests who engaged only nominally in any sort of apostolate. Living within the circle of their families, these priests turned their hearts from those who most needed care, concern, and compassion.[29]

Alphonsus, however, was convinced that although there was a great need, he was not the person to begin such a work. After all, he was still a young priest. He sincerely pointed out to Falcoia his own lack of experience and lack of leadership ability.

Two factors bothered Alphonsus. First, it seemed to him entirely possible that Maria Celeste was guided by her own imagination rather than by the will of God. Second, he was already committed to intense missionary work in the Propaganda. Prudence did not dictate abandoning a path of proven success for a bypath of possible good; and Alphonsus was a prudent man. In any case, he would do nothing until he had time to pray earnestly for the light to see God's will in the situation, and to consult his director, Father Pagano.

Pagano reinforced all the reasons considered by Alphonsus for resisting the plans of Falcoia and added a few more. How could the young missionary possibly do more for God, reasoned Pagano. Would the proposed Congregation ever materialize? And finally, the physical strength of the young priest had already been drawn to the breaking point twice in his short career. The demands made upon his stamina by the proposed apostolate were too great to risk. Pagano concluded: "It is your duty to stay as you are, and to cease thinking about changing your state of life."[30]

Alphonsus should have found peace in his confessor's direction. Had it not, after all, voiced the same convictions Alphonsus had found himself expressing to Falcoia? And yet, he was unable to put the plan out of his mind. Time and time again he felt called to reach out to the poor of the mountains and the poor of the countryside. When he tried to find peace in a few hours of sleep at the end of a trying day, his mind and heart turned to the ragged clusters of foul-smelling goatherds who had camped on his doorstep at Santa Maria dei Monti. They stood there and waited for him, waiting to hear that Christ loved them, waiting to realize he cared. What was God saying to him? What was God's will?

Finally, he could stand it no longer. Returning to Father Pagano, he told him that he was unable to put the project out of his mind. This time, instead of restating his original objections, Pagano expressed the belief that the idea of the future Congregation seemed to be from God, and told Alphonsus to look into the matter further.

As a safeguard, Pagano suggested that Alphonsus seek the additional advice of a few trusted friends. Ordinarily, the first choice of the young missionary would have been Matthew Ripa, head of the Chinese College and longtime friend of Falcoia. But Ripa was on the way to Rome to try to secure papal approbation for his own Institute. So Alphonsus turned to two religious whose opinions he valued highly: Father Vincent Cutica, the superior of the Vincentians who had preached the retreat that began his "conversion," and Father Dominic Manulio, provincial of the Society of Jesus. Both men, after careful examination of the facts of the case and prayerful consideration, agreed that the proposed Congregation would add to the glory of God, and advised Alphonsus to pursue the vocation that seemed to be so clearly mapped out for him.[31]

Four men whose opinions Alphonsus valued more than those of anyone else in Naples now encouraged him to undertake the burden of organizing the Institute: Pagano, Cutica, Manulio, and Falcoia. And yet Alphonsus was afraid, afraid of his own unworthiness.

Perhaps, he thought, it would help to examine the details of Maria Celeste's vision more closely. After all, he had only a secondhand version of it from Falcoia's viewpoint; and the lawyer in him demanded firsthand testimony. So he set out for Scala with two of his dearest friends, Mazzini and Mannarini, but without telling them the purpose of his visit. He somehow hoped to put his fears to rest, but he traveled with a heavy heart.

Alphonsus confronted Maria Celeste, convinced of his own inability to carry out what was asked of him. Mazzini supplies us with the following account of what happened:

> I was in the chapel while the servant of God was hearing the confessions of the religious. Suddenly I noticed that he raised his voice in an unusual way. He seemed to be contesting what his penitent was saying. The confessions over, we entered the house in which we were living. There he shut himself in his room. I could hear his weeping from my cell. It was the dinner hour and I took the liberty of knocking on his door to remind him of it. Seeing him in tears, I asked the cause of his distress. "Perhaps the argument you have just been having with one of the religious," I remarked, "has something to do with it. If it does not fall under the seal of confession, tell me the cause of such a painful discussion and it may help to restore peace to your soul." "Just think," he answered, "Maria Celeste says that I must abandon Naples to found a new Congregation at Scala to reach the country dis-

tricts. Such, she tells me, is the will of God. It is beyond my strength. Besides, you know all my works in Naples, the missions in which I have to take part, and all the affairs in which I am involved. It is this which troubles me, and crushes me with anxious fears. I cannot see my way to undertake this work, yet if I do not undertake it I am afraid of resisting the will of God."

I tried to console my friend and to rouse him from his depression. "Courage," I said, "there is no need for you to torment yourself in this way. We do not know for certain what is the will of God; let us wait until it is quite clear." "Then again," he exclaimed, pursuing his own train of thought, "where would you have me look for companions?" "As for that," I replied, "I myself will be your first companion. So let us sit down to dinner for it is time and we will leave the care of arranging everything to God." These words calmed him a little. He followed me to the refectory where naturally we continued the conversation that had begun.[32]

When Mannarini heard of the plan to found the new Congregation he also offered himself as a member. The loyalty of his two dear friends helped to calm Alphonsus for the time being.

But calm never seemed to rule the life of Alphonsus for very long. After asking Maria Celeste to put her experience on paper so that Father Pagano would have better grounds for judgment, he left once again to preach a series of missions for the Propaganda. Months passed with no new developments as Alphonsus preached mission after mission throughout Apulia, Nardo, and Foggia. Earthquakes shook southern Italy and as the missionaries traveled from place to place, they encountered many who had lost everything they possessed in the quakes that buried whole towns in rubble.[33]

When the weary apostle finally returned to Naples, he did not find the haven he had hoped for. In his absence the story of Maria Celeste's vision had reached the hearing of his superiors in the Propaganda and the members of the Chinese College. Both groups jeered the young priest who had been "hypnotized" by the imaginings of a hysterical woman into abandoning an important work of the Church. It seemed obvious to all that Alphonsus was willing to betray a brilliant future for a misguided adventure founded on sand.

One by one they appealed to his logic, his prudence, his wit. Alphonsus patiently answered each one of them: "You are mistaken: I follow the Gospel and not a vision."

"How can you possibly hope to succeed?" asked Canon Gizzio.

"One who trusts in God may hope for everything from him," answered Alphonsus. Gizzio threw up his hands in frustration. It seemed obvious that Alphonsus had suddenly become proud, obstinate, and unreasonable. Many of his colleagues agreed completely with Gizzio.

After hours of discussion that always ended in the same blind alley, Gizzio finally urged Alphonsus to consult his own spiritual director, Father Fiorillo, a respected Dominican priest whom he hoped would succeed where Gizzio had failed. The weary missionary had already consulted three authorities he considered both holy and learned, and had received encouragement from all of them. Gizzio knew very well that Alphonsus had accepted the decisions of Father Pagano all of his life. Why should he now seek the counsel of a priest to whom he had never even spoken?

In spite of all the reasons Alphonsus stated for not seeking the advice of still another person, he mentioned Gizzio's proposal to Pagano. To his surprise his director answered: "Go to Father Fiorillo. If he approves of the work, I approve of it too: if he decides that God does not will it, neither do I."[34]

The whole future of the missionary now rested on the opinion of a man whom he had never met. After making an appointment, Alphonsus presented the facts of the case as clearly and objectively as possible, showing Fiorillo the written account of the vision of Maria Celeste and explaining the circumstances for and against the proposed work. He pleaded with the Dominican simply to make known to him the will of God. Fiorillo shifted in his chair and replied slowly: "In a similar case, Saint Louis Bertrand asked Saint Teresa to give him six months to consider. I ask the same of you."

"Take six months, take a year if you wish," replied Alphonsus.

"I will wait for your decision." For months Alphonsus had already been praying for the light to see God's will: a few months did not seem like a penance to him now.

Within eight days, however, Father Fiorillo sent for Don Liguori. Embracing him, he pronounced: "Courage my son. The work you contemplate is God's work. Great persecutions are before you but do not be afraid. God will be your aid." When he was informed of Fiorillo's decision, Father Pagano gave the work his own blessings and from that moment Alphonsus could not look back.[35]

Meanwhile, on July 25 Matthew Ripa returned from Rome in high spirits having finally succeeded in obtaining formal approbation of his Institute. Although his community was still small and still struggled with great poverty, he knew he could count on his subjects' and supporters' loyalty and willingness to sacrifice, and was confident that they were destined to do great work for God.

But Ripa had been in the house a very short time before he was informed of the plans of Alphonsus. Appealing to Alphonsus as a friend rather than as an opponent, he tried to persuade him to alter his plans.

> I demonstrated to him by numerous arguments that he ought not to leave the certain good he was doing in our Church and congregation for the very uncertain good he hoped to do in an institute which did not yet even exist. I put before his eyes the harm he would do us, especially if he took away our mainstay, Mannarini. I declared, moreover, that his plan seemed to me unreasonable because if he wished to devote himself to preaching or to the instruction of the young he would find abundant means with us to exercise this two-fold ministry, since our society had for its object to preach the Gospel to the ends of the earth, and to open schools even for the pagans. But all my reasoning failed to move him. He only answered: "I am absolutely certain about my vocation."[36]

In desperation, Ripa appealed to Falcoia, pouring into a single letter every objection he could possibly think of to prevent the

step Alphonsus was ready to take. Falcoia's letter answered each
of his objections in turn.

> You tell me that a director may be mistaken, but I
> answer that God is faithful to His promises and never
> refuses to enlighten those whom He has placed in the world
> to be the light of souls. Otherwise, what sure means should
> we have of knowing God's will? And it is by following
> this rule that Alphonsus will never go astray.
>
> You condemn me as though I were seeking to destroy
> your Congregation. But after all, what have you to fear?
> Has God's arm been shortened or is He unable to sustain
> your house and to build another one too? Let us leave
> things to the good God: the work He begins today does
> not destroy but rather consolidates what He had done
> yesterday.
>
> The new Institute will not stand, you say. If it comes
> from God it will stand in spite of storms. If it does not come
> from God it will fall, and then what harm can it do you?
>
> You are taking precious subjects away from me. I wish,
> dear Father, that we put a little more confidence in God
> and less in human instruments. The Congregation of the
> Pious Workers had scarcely been founded when it lost
> four excellent subjects, who left it to found four other
> Congregations. The venerable Father Caraffa was not
> troubled by that, and he was right. God sent him new
> workers to replace those who went away. I beg you then,
> dear Father, not to allow yourself to be deceived by the
> evil one, who wishes to make use of you to create ob-
> stacles for our holy enterprize.[37]

Both Pagano and Fiorillo, meanwhile, found themselves subject to the same criticism that was being leveled at Alphonsus.
After all, they had encouraged him in his madness when they should
have had the wisdom to see the possible consequences. Their own
reputations were in danger, and their effectiveness in dealing with
their own colleagues was becoming hampered. A solution to the
difficulty had to be found.

Father Pagano, after thinking of several possible ways to solve the dilemma, asked Alphonsus to consider taking Monsignor Falcoia as his spiritual director. The reasons for the move seemed logical; after all, Falcoia was to play an important part in the future of the Congregation, while Pagano was completely removed from any involvement in the work itself. Alphonsus agreed that there were many objective advantages in the step. But Father Pagano had been the only director he had ever known. He knew his moods and fears, his anxieties and his great desires. He had followed him without question when the future seemed little more than a black abyss. He promised to pray about the advice, but he knew that he did not want to take it.

Beginning a novena in preparation for the feast of the Assumption, he asked Our Lady of Ransom to join him in praying to know her Son's will in this matter. On the feast itself, kneeling before the Madonna, as he had so very many times before, he finally knew for certain that God willed that he follow Pagano's advice. Writing to Falcoia, he promised to follow him in all questions of conscience and all matters concerning the Congregation. Later, he sealed the promise with a vow.[38]

Falcoia blessed his decision and told him that preparations were being made at Scala for the beginning of the work. He advised Alphonsus to bear the persecution he was enduring patiently and to place the future completely in God's hands.

Early in November, a young priest traveled slowly down the dirt road leading from Naples to the coastal town of Scala. The sleeves and hem of his dusty cassock were raveled and beginning to shred. The donkey he rode bore no resemblance whatever to the matched team of black horses that once pulled the carriage of the famed Don Liguori, lawyer and nobleman. He had left friends and family, wealth and reputation. Now he was going to work for abandoned souls as Jesus had done.

CHAPTER 4

The End of the Beginning

On the first of November 1732, Alphonsus Liguori reached Scala.[1] Two years that had passed since he first climbed the winding road melted in his mind. The rocks and sea were changeless, and he found himself consciously absorbing some of their peace.

The preparations to receive him were simple. The tiny guesthouse of the convent, which he had occupied while giving former retreats, had been turned over to Alphonsus and his companions until they could make permanent arrangements. As he crossed the threshold into the bare interior, he knew what to expect; a chapel had been created in one of the larger rooms and it was flanked by three miniature cells. A fourth room served as a temporary community room. The furnishings could be listed without taxing his memory: a few chairs, wooden beds, and used pots and pans began and ended the inventory.

Three companions greeted him: Vincent Mannarini, John Baptist Donato, and Peter Romano. Mannarini had been the first to arrive at Scala, since Matthew Ripa had asked him to leave the college immediately when he refused to abandon plans to join Alphonsus.[2] He held degrees in both law and theology and had already achieved the reputation of an effective and zealous missionary. Mannarini was also responsible for the presence of John Baptist Donato, who had first learned of the new community through his friend and fellow Calabrian. Donato had left a community devoted to spreading devotion to the Blessed Sacrament in order to join Alphonsus.

Don Peter Romano was already well known at Scala. He had served as regular confessor of the sisters of San Salvatore, and through this association, had been well informed of the plans for the new Institute almost from the beginning.

Four other recruits had pledged to join them but as yet were unable to free themselves from their obligations. Mazzini, the fourth priest of the band, promised to be the first to follow Alphonsus, but obedience to his director kept him in Naples long after the rest arrived. More than any of the others, perhaps, he desired to be there—and wasn't.

The other three all intended to join the Institute as lay brothers: Cesare Sportelli, Sylvester Tosquez, and Vitus Curtius.

Sportelli was a layman and distinguished lawyer. Falcoia had been his director since boyhood and now, at the age of thirty, he expressed eagerness to join the new community. It would take a little time to withdraw from his obligations as the agent of the Marquis de Vasto, but he promised to join the group as soon as possible.

Vitus Curtius, the Marquis de Vasto's secretary, was perhaps the most colorful of the original seven members of the Institute. His past was a careless mosaic of pride, arrogance, and adventure. The sword he wore at his side was more than the symbol of his social rank. Alphonsus himself, when writing a short biography of the lay brother many years later, tells us:

> On one occasion amongst others, he felt so offended by a doctor that he shot him. Another time he had the boldness to fire at a military officer; but God did not permit him to have the misfortune of hitting his mark.[3]

Through the efforts of Cesare Sportelli, Curtius had withdrawn gradually from his self-centered world of violence. But the real reason for finding himself in the tiny house at Scala was, strangely enough, a recurring dream which he had mentioned to Sportelli. "I saw myself at the foot of a steep mountain and a number of priests were trying to reach the top. I wanted to follow them, but every time I tried to take a step forward, I slipped and fell back. I tried again and again but to my disgust I kept slipping and falling back until at last one of the priests, moved by compassion took me by the hand and helped me to climb the mountain."[4] Both friends laughed a little at the strange dream and promptly forgot it.

The seventh of the original recruits to the Congregation was another distinguished lawyer, Sylvester Tosquez, Inspector General of Customs. His background was one of wealth and influence, and he was considered capable of filling any one of several high government posts; yet his interests ran along antithetical lines. Spending his free time in studying mysticism, he soon acquired a facility in discussing topics dealing with the contemplative life. Knowledge, however, was gleaned more from research than experience, a fact that he was, unfortunately, the first to overlook. The logic of his approach demanded that he somehow surrender his legal interests to embrace the religious life but no existing order seemed to appeal to him.

Six months before the community was to convene at Scala, however, his friend Mannarini told him about plans to join a community of "active contemplatives" who would preach the gospel to the poor. Mannarini ended the conversation by inviting Tosquez to join them. Instantly the lawyer accepted the invitation.

When Tosquez offered his gifts to Alphonsus, he was sent to Falcoia to discuss the sincerity of his vocation.

After a single short interview with Tosquez, Falcoia gave permission to visit the convent at Scala to speak to the religious personally, especially with Sister Maria Celeste, since Tosquez seemed particularly interested in her vision of the future community. The bishop was soon to regret his hasty decision.

The lawyer was enchanted with the convent. His deep interest in mystical phenomena prompted him to extend his afternoon's visit to several days, during which time he interviewed each of the sisters separately and spent several hours conversing with Sister Maria Celeste.

His position was that of a layman seeking admission to a future Congregation, yet his natural gifts of conversation and broad background of spiritual reading encouraged him, in his enthusiasm, to assume a role that was not his to assume. We can gauge from a letter Maria Celeste wrote to Alphonsus at this time something of his initial effect on her.

Tosquez will be your counselor. When God lavishes all the gifts of nature and of grace upon a man, it means that he wishes to make him not only a saint himself but a guide in the paths of sanctity.[5]

A note from Sister Mary Columba that arrived about the same time helped Alphonsus to realize that Tosquez was going to be a problem. She referred to him in passing as "a man unduly attached to his own opinion."[6]

Unfortunately, Tosquez encountered Maria Celeste while she was undergoing a serious crisis of conscience. For a long time Celeste had witnessed the change Falcoia was making in the rules and constitutions that she believed God had revealed to her. She told him repeatedly that she felt that he was distorting something that could not be substantially changed without compromising the will of God.

Both Falcoia and Alphonsus agreed that if the rule was inspired by God, no substantial change should be made. But Alphonsus assured her that the changes made in the outward form of the constitutions demanded by canonical custom in no way detracted from their substance. Falcoia, believing that he was teaching Maria Celeste necessary lessons in humility, answered her severely whenever she objected to alterations he presented, reminding her harshly that her vision could well be only an illusion, and telling her that she had no right to judge a private revelation.

The thought tormented her. *Was* she the victim of her imagination after all? When she faced God in prayer she was certain that she was not. But when she faced Falcoia her peace was always shattered. Countless times she had been tempted to request permission to change her director in hopes of restoring her peace, but she had yet to act.

Tosquez inspired her confidence and she shared with him her state of anxiety about Falcoia, her director. Impressed by her obvious state of holiness, he agreed with everything she said. She was right, he assured her; Falcoia was distorting the rule that God had revealed to her, and to restore her peace of soul she should change directors.

Before Alphonsus was informed of the situation the convent

had split into two opposing centers of loyalty. One group sided with Celeste and Tosquez in opposing the interference of Falcoia; and the second defended the authority of the bishop. Alphonsus immediately informed Falcoia of the situation that seemed to have arisen and urged him to settle the matter immediately.

Falcoia visited Scala briefly and convinced himself that the situation was not that serious. Writing to Alphonsus, he assured him:

> Do not be alarmed. All the religious, including Maria Celeste, are perfectly submissive to me. Tosquez, too, shows himself to be well disposed. The religious life will soon break him in.[7]

On Sunday, November 9, 1732, Alphonsus, Mannarini, Romano, and Donato walked to the cathedral of Scala to inaugurate solemnly the Institute.[8] Falcoia celebrated Mass, and together they chanted the *Te Deum*.

The days that followed were far from peaceful ones for the young Congregation. Conferences were held each day to determine the content of the rules and constitutions of the new Institute and to agree on the scope of the work they were about to undertake.

The group, as small as it was, could agree on only one point: their rule would be essentially an adaptation of the one already drawn up for the convent of San Salvatore, since both communities were formed from the same root. But any attempt to discuss the scope of the apostolate, the habit of the community, or the extent of their community poverty led nowhere. Each member had his own idea of religious life and how it should be lived, and without an authority to settle a point, when agreement seemed otherwise impossible, discussion ended in pointless disagreements.

The problem then, rested firmly on a single question: Who should be the final authority? Tosquez, Mannarini, and Donato rejected Falcoia's interpretation of the rule, agreeing with Maria Celeste that he had ignored direct revelation from God on the subject. They were almost ready to follow Alphonsus because Maria Celeste's revelation had clearly pictured him at their head, but they hesitated because they feared he might later become a pawn for Falcoia.

Alphonsus stood alone in defense of Falcoia's authority over the work. In the face of such clear opposition, Falcoia advised Alphonsus to discontinue discussion until tempers cooled. He made Alphonsus promise at the same time, to stand by his position even if he had to remain alone. Alphonsus wrote in his personal diary:

> Today, November 6, I vow never to give up the work unless my director obliges me to. Further, I vow never to consent to the smallest doubts as to my vocation and to obey Msgr. Falcoia in all things.[9]

Differences of opinion plagued the future of the Institute, but daily life reflected the willingness of the members to sacrifice their own comfort in order to strengthen the work. Missions consumed the energies of the few priests among them and tested their ability to work together for the good of those they had come to serve.

While preaching near Tremonti, the group was visited by Tosquez, who arrived from Naples. Although he stayed only four days before returning to his duties at Naples, Alphonsus was struck by a change that seemed to have come over the young man. After his departure he concluded that Tosquez was a humble and obedient man at heart and that he might eventually become a loyal member of the community.

Alphonsus was so encouraged by his own changed judgment about Tosquez, in fact, that he decided to write to Maria Celeste. He spoke to her not as a director but as a friend.

March, 1733

Live Jesus, Mary, Joseph and Teresa!
Celeste,
I am answering your last letter which I received at the same time as that of Msgr. Falcoia…Judging from what Monsignor writes to me and from what I hear of Don Silvestro, affairs are now in the best condition. The latter continues to remain on intimate terms as formerly. There is, however, one thorn that pierces my heart and causes

me great anguish: it deprives me, too, of my night's sleep and it is, my dear Celeste, the thought of you. I see that during this trouble between us, you have not uttered one sentiment breathing humility.

Especially in your last letter, I noticed how you address me and how you sign yourself; I perceived, too, how little you care whether I believe you or not...I know that you bear me no ill will, but judging from the altered style of your letter, it appears to me that you do retain some ill feelings towards me. I do not say that I deserve to see you humble yourself before me. I confess that I am not worthy even to sit at your feet for I know your life and I know my own. But I do not on account of this despair of loving Jesus as you do; He will grant me this in His infinite mercy.

What I wish to say is that I should like to see in a soul so united to God and so favored by Him, as is your soul, the profoundest humility, for the greater our humility is the more intimate is our union with God: the one is ever in proportion to the other. Humility, however, does not consist at all in *saying* "I am a wretch, I deserve much worse than this"; no, it consists in having a low opinion of one's self and in knowing how to humble one's self most before him who most despises us. I would have desired this humility for you, even though I should have had reason to ask for other things. But up to now I have not seen it in you, and this is the thorn that torments me.

Understand now that in matters that relate to the welfare of the Institute, I can quickly rid myself of your intrigues by laying the whole matter before Falcoia; however, I have not done so, as it seems to me a kind of treachery to reveal the situation to Falcoia when I myself, though troubled and disgusted, can remedy the situation by writing to you. You cannot imagine what great pain it causes me to treat anyone harshly, especially as I believe that more may be done by gentleness than by harshness.

If perhaps, through lack of reflection and through indiscreet zeal, I have gone beyond the bounds of modera-

tion and you, consequently, feel yourself offended, I beg
your pardon now and always and beg you to pardon me.
If I were allowed, I would kiss your feet a thousand times
for having so treated a beloved spouse of Jesus Christ. If
Msgr. Falcoia gives me permission, I will beg your pardon publicly before all. But still I want to see you as humble
as I wish you to be.

And is my soul then of so much importance to you?
(she had written). My dear Celeste, do not speak like that
to me for it sounds like great ingratitude: the union of
our souls in Jesus Christ is too intimate for that. Do you
not know that the interests of your soul have become mine?
And this is not my work but God's work; but I must desire the same perfection for you that I wish to obtain for
myself.

I am looking for reasons to excuse you and to calm
my alarm at seeing your lack of humility, and I am trying to
convince myself that you have not considered the matter
sufficiently. Perhaps you have a good reason for treating
me like this but the thorn still continues to torment me.

I do not call you daughter that you may not think I
am claiming what is not mine....[10]

This letter, however, failed to stem the approaching crisis. Writing to Alphonsus, Celeste tried to explain her motive for seeking a
director other than Falcoia, a letter written after the fact.

I had long desired to change my director for the following reasons: for five years, that is to say, ever since I
revealed to him the divine communication concerning the
Institute, Msgr. Falcoia had been greatly puzzled about
me. His mind remained in darkness as to the paths by
which God was leading me so I concluded that he was no
longer the channel of the divine will in my regard. Subsequently, he would interpret everything I told him in all
simplicity and in the candor of my soul, in a sinister sense,
completely contrary to my thought, and this used to plunge
me into an abyss of uneasiness and suffering. And as he no

longer discerned my internal state with clearness, I realized that he could never help me find the peace for which I longed. I asked his permission, therefore, to consult another director, especially in important matters, but he formally forbade me to do so. He attributed this desire to pride and said things to me that made me cry whole days and nights. Still I did not open my mind to anyone until the moment when I saw my director, by his doubts and difficulties, go against the lights given by God on the Institute, and so cause division among those who were to form part of it. Then after mature consideration, and with no other object than that of pleasing God and securing my peace of mind, I felt obliged to seek other counsel for my guidance....[11]

In the hopes of persuading Celeste to abandon opposition to the leadership of Falcoia, Alphonsus outlined the principles upon which his own loyalty was based. His fears for the sanctity of Celeste as well as the future of the Congregation are apparent in one of the longest letters ever written during his long missionary life.

March, 1733

Praised be Jesus, Mary, Joseph and Teresa!
Celeste, my beloved Sister in Jesus Christ and our Mother Mary,

...Tell me, Celeste, why have you left Msgr. Falcoia, who is so saintly and so enlightened as you yourself have often told me? You know that God himself has given him to you as your director. What defect have you now discovered in him? Has he perhaps cast you into an abyss? Have you left him because he disturbs you by humbling you? But, my dear Sister, do you not see that this course is absolutely necessary to conquer your high spirit and to prevent you from becoming attached to your own judgment? This is a fault that was perceived in you not only by Msgr. Falcoia but also by Don Bartolomeo Caracas (her first director) and by others who were acquainted with you. Who has approved of the step you have taken in leaving Falcoia? Have you perhaps received light from God? Are the effects sufficient signs of the correctness of your step? And who has approved of these lights and of this sense of peace?

The most experienced and cautious masters of the spiritual life can be deceived on this point and you wish to have certainty in the matter by taking counsel with yourself? But has perhaps Don Silvestro given his approval? If you suspect Falcoia because he has humbled you, you have greater reason to mistrust the judgment of Don Silvestro who, as you know, places you above Saint Teresa and sings your praises everywhere, even at Vienna. He approves of everything, even of his entire dependence on you, a thing which, above all others, a spiritual director should guard against, if he wishes to guide a soul properly and to keep it humble.

O my dear Celeste, how Don Silvestro has caused you to lose the spirit of humility! How has he aided you in wedding yourself to your own judgment! Where is that Celeste whom I used to know? How has this ruin happened? I feel the touch of death whenever I think of it. Who has so fascinated you? Where is your former prompt obedience to Superiors? Where is that beautiful spirit of humility that prompted you to desire to be despised by all?

Now, however, having abandoned the practice of obedience, you are trying to gain the respect and approval of all under the false pretense of seeking the glory of God. God does not need your self-defense to promote his glory. When he sees you truly humble, he will defend you and your work. You already understand what I mean.

Let me tell you that Don Silvestro, whose fine teachings on obedience you perhaps have followed, is very much prone to doctrinal error. He has followed many errors in Moral Theology but I shall not go into them here. It is enough to know that he had the audacity to insist, as you perhaps have already heard, that all who were under the spiritual direction of Falcoia were damned....

Falcoia is partial and Don Silvestro is not so? Celeste,

give this great pleasure to God—to leave Don Silvestro. I know that you will have to do great violence to yourself; but the greater the violence, the longer will be the step towards holiness. Tell me, if God wishes you to leave Don Silvestro, are you willing to make the sacrifice? My beloved Celeste in Jesus Christ, who does not clearly see that you are deluded, and what is worse by far voluntarily so? What excuse will you have for Jesus Christ on the day of judgment after hearing the truth from so many persons? To this you will perhaps reply: "That is my affair." Well, then, let us pass to the other point—the affairs of the Institute.

It is certain that the rules noted down by you need a thousand and one explanations. Do you not yourself remember telling me when I first went to the convent that Falcoia acted wisely in sifting the divine elements from the human, as there were many things in the rules which owed their origin to self-will? You moreover agreed to this in regard to the Institute for men when, before the opening of the foundation, I went to Scala to call upon you. We surveyed the matter and came to an agreement. Besides the countless explanations of the rules, there are many other points and constitutions which are to be treated separately; as, for example, the schools, the missions, the houses of study, the different exercises to be given by us, the occupations which are permitted or prohibited, the academies, the meetings, etc., so that the same observances may ever flourish in the Congregation.

Now who is to give these explanations and constitutions? Don Vincenzo (Mannarini) and I have no practical experience of community life; I am moreover an ignoramus. Don Silvestro (Tosquez) is less practical than we. Don Giovanni (Donato) still has an attachment to his old Rule; hence, as you know, he is resolutely opposed to the recitation of Office in choir—a point which is so essential. In short, he would like to introduce his old Rule among us.

Furthermore, if we should leave Falcoia in order to

agree among ourselves upon the rules, Don Silvestro would most certainly wish to play the role of director and infallible interpreter of your revelation. He is used to playing the teacher and not the disciple, and woe to the man who should dare to contradict him in this matter, as experience has shown me that he wishes to rule in everything. And if, scarcely having entered the monastery, he undertook as a layman the guidance of several Sisters who now, according to their own confession, find themselves emerging from the darkness after leaving his spiritual direction. If I say, having but entered, he wishes that permission should be obtained from him when a letter was to be written to Falcoia, what would he do if we should forsake Falcoia? I already believe that it would be your aim after we should have left Falcoia to induce us all to follow Don Silvestro blindly as an oracle and to depend on him entirely as you do. If it were God's will I would do so, but at present I do not feel that inspiration.

The only way to establish anything on a solid basis is to place ourselves entirely in the hands of one man, and having communicated to him our ideas, to follow his counsels and directions. He must be a man of experience with a practical knowledge of community life, missions, and other spiritual exercises: he must be a man of enlightened spirit and, finally, one who will solve all doubts and questions without appeal. In this way charity and unity will be preserved among us....

My Sister, let me tell you once and for all that I have not entered the Institute to become its head and director, or to take precedence in anything, as you seem to insinuate, or to please men.... You know that I have surrendered myself entirely into the hands of Falcoia and so I hope to live and die under the yoke of obedience. If you choose to follow another route, goodbye until we meet again at the place for which you are striving....I tell you that I have no intention of deserting Falcoia, even though all—if such a thing were possible—should place themselves entirely in my hands. Do you not see that it is far better to give up one's vocation than to give up the practice of obedience, that is, if a true vocation could exist without obedience. To conclude, I am content to leave the Institute and to practice obedience rather than remain in the Institute and give up obedience.

My God, what a terrible hallucination you have been laboring under, Celeste! This happens when an enlightened soul, through some fault of her own, falls into a delusion; this I dare to say of you and I add that a miracle on the part of God is necessary to open your eyes to the light. See how disunited we are and know that you are the cause of this disunion.

Celeste, I am speaking to you in the name of God. Consider well that you, by your obstinacy, are devoting to destruction a work that is not yours but God's. True it is that neither you nor all the men in the world can ruin the work of God if he wishes to prevent it; I am inclined to think that if you remain stubborn, Our Lord will aid us more, for when there shall be no longer any talk about lights and revelations, we shall more easily obtain approbation from Rome. But as for you, if you appear before Jesus Christ burdened with the charge of having tried to ruin his work, what will become of your poor soul? If I be excluded from the Institute, as you keep repeating, I confess that I deserve to be excluded and am content, provided I am allowed to practice obedience; but I beg you, at the same time, to understand that neither you nor Don Silvestro can expel me from the Institute: that is God's affair and he needs neither you nor Don Silvestro. I consider myself unmistakenly called to the Institute, for obedience has told me so. As for you, Celeste, I see you on the brink of disaster and I shall bitterly regret your loss if you do not turn back.

My dear Celeste, do listen to me: humble yourself; the Lord will certainly enlighten you if you humble yourself; obey your Superiors and you will fall into no error; Falcoia is holy and meek. Do not for a moment imagine that he wishes you ill. If you humble yourself before him, you will be dearer to him than at first. Be resigned to the will of God and pray; otherwise your prayer will be of no service to you, all your reasons will be passions, and your revelations will be imagination and delusion. If you do not care to listen to me and to Falcoia, consult other unprejudiced men. Seek other assistance; do not walk blindly on the road to destruction; seek the advice of others, not to find material for reply but to discover and embrace the truth with your whole heart.

Believe me, dear Celeste, all that I have written I have written because I love you in Jesus Christ; if you wish me evil you do me a great wrong. May Jesus and Mary induce me to do the will of God!

My letter is finished but I feel it necessary to say a few more words. My dear Celeste, pardon me if I conclude by speaking too frankly. Do you not realize the fact that you are attached to Don Silvestro and that he returns this feeling? I do not say that you are sinning thereby, but am I not right in saying that there is a great deal of this earth in such an affection? You do not seek God alone in Don Silvestro, but look also for something else which is not God. Take care lest by following Don Silvestro you voluntarily place yourself in danger of losing God. To sum up: So much is certain, if you follow Falcoia you will surely become a saint; if you follow Don Silvestro you will certainly not sanctify yourself and only God knows whether you will be saved.

Live Jesus and Mary!

Alphonso Liguori,
a poor sinner.[12]

Celeste did not seem to follow Alphonsus' advice, although it could not help but leave an impression on her. "After receiving this letter," she says, "seeing myself abandoned by all, sick in body and lonely in heart, I abandoned myself entirely into the hands of Divine Providence and waited, with no lights other than those of faith, until God should be pleased to let me know his will."[13]

The crisis within the Institute was growing worse, and the

strain on the heart of Alphonsus seemed at times more than he could bear. Writing to Falcoia, he revealed his discouragement.

> I thank God for giving me strength in the midst of these storms to resist the temptation to lose heart. This is my reward after having left the whole world—my family, my friends, and archbishop—in order to obey the voice of God! O Father, do not abandon me, for without your help I do not know what is to become of me.[14]

It seemed humanly impossible to gather the shreds of promise that had clothed the work in its beginnings, but Alphonsus refused to give up hope. His close friend and early support, Mannarini, was preaching a mission at Tramonti with the rest of the priests of the Institute when Alphonsus sent him an urgent notice to return to Scala. On Good Friday a reply arrived that might have broken the spirit of another man.

> I shall return to Scala but only to put my affairs in order. Our Colleagues of Teano (Donato's former community) with whom we are in contact have decided to join us. Don Silvestro will also form one of our number and will take upon himself the task of providing the funds necessary for our new establishment. If you will come with us—and this is what we all earnestly beg of you—our dearest wishes will be fulfilled. Our most ardent desire is never to be separated from you but to live together united in the peace of Jesus Christ. Should you decide otherwise, it will be a source of bitter regret to us, but I hope that Our Lord and his Blessed Mother will not permit this.[15]

After only six months at Scala his coworkers were leaving him to suffer alone. The people who had warned him not to give up everything in order to follow this folly seized this situation as only another indication of his self-will. As Alphonsus stood in the doorway gazing across the sea to a solid horizon, he could not help but wonder if they were really right. Before his death he would look back at this Good Friday afternoon and remember it as one of the most severe temptations in his life. Only the vow that he had resolutely recorded in his personal diary kept him from turning his back and walking away from the ruins of the Congregation himself. He stood and prepared to celebrate his dark Easter alone.

Falcoia did not seem to share his depression, but perhaps it was simply that he could not feel the wounds from a distance. In answer to the news of the apparent collapse of the Institute, he outlined the following opinion:

> ...You are gaining more than you are losing in this separation. In the first place, it establishes you more solidly in obedience; in the second, with the disappearance of your colleagues, great obstacles to the progress of the work also disappear; and finally, had your companions not gone away of their own accord, it would have become necessary to send them away, and it is better to be abandoned by others than to get rid of them.[16]

Alphonsus traveled to Castellamare to try to pick up the pieces of the project and plan for the future. In his absence, events at Scala became even worse.

Celeste had been confined to her cell and prevented from participating in community exercises. Following the schism within the ranks of the community, the supporters of Falcoia among the sisters of San Salvatore, including the superior, pointed to Maria Celeste as the cause of the whole situation. If she had not refused to follow Falcoia's direction, they insisted, others would have had no reason to question his authority.

On April 20, writing to her confessor, Pedro Romano, she repeated the same reasons for seeking a new director that she had tried earlier to explain to Alphonsus. She went on to say:

> I protest now before God and man that I no longer occupy myself with the Institute, the rules, the fathers, or the sisters. I renounce for guidance all supernatural lights— or even the lights of my own mind; I renounce my own judgment and give myself up entirely to the light of faith for my guidance. I renounce myself to attach myself to

Jesus who alone is the happiness of my soul. I was wrong in thinking that Msgr. Falcoia, by talking of me as a visionary, was compromising the work of God—as if God could be hurt by only disgrace. Be kind enough to tell him and the whole Community that they will be doing me a favor by publishing my imperfections and sins, for I shall thus be able to repair by my own humiliation all the honor of which I have deprived God....[17]

Meanwhile, acting on the advice of Falcoia, the superior informed Celeste that she would be dismissed from the community unless she agreed to three conditions:

1. to end all correspondence with Tosquez
2. to sign with her own hand Falcoia's version of the rule
3. to bind herself by vow to entrust to Falcoia the direction of her conscience[18]

During the time that was permitted to consider her answer, Celeste was visited by one of her brothers, a learned Jesuit priest. After listening to her account of the whole situation, he advised that she was not required to take the vow that was demanded of her. In fact, he insisted that in her present state of mind it might even be very harmful.

Celeste appeared before her sisters with a heavy heart. Her superior formally read the three conditions that had been put to her and called upon her to agree to each in turn. To the first, she answered wearily that she had no more reason to write to Tosquez and promised never to communicate with him again. To the second, she agreed to sign the rule although she did not feel worthy to do so. When the third condition was read, Celeste bowed her head and answered sadly that she was prevented and would always be prevented by serious motives of conscience from binding herself by such a vow.[19]

In spite of the objections of those who supported her, the superior solemnly declared Sister Maria Celeste expelled from the community. The following morning, May 25, 1733, Celeste left the convent of Scala. She was eventually to enter a convent at

Nocera at the request of the bishop, and her cause has been presented for beatification.

What would have happened if Alphonsus himself had been at Scala? Would he not have agreed that Celeste should not be forced to take a vow that she felt violated her conscience? She had agreed willingly to conditions that affected the work of others and had removed herself from any further part in the work. And she had finally voiced the humility that Alphonsus had desired so much to see in her. Certainly, he would not have asked more.

The aftermath of the expulsion of Maria Celeste from the convent at Scala engulfed the entire project. The reputations of everyone connected with it were publicly questioned. The work seemed ruined. Even Alphonsus was ordered to leave Scala, and the pope forbade the bishops of Scala and Castellamare to have anything further to do with it for the time being. Preachers in Naples even used Alphonsus as an example of what can happen to a good man who relies too much on his own judgment.

The only friend who did not seem to turn against him was Cardinal Pignatelli, Archbishop of Naples, who asked Alphonsus to visit him so that he could examine the facts of the situation for himself. Alphonsus went but it cost him a great deal to enter Naples where everyone he knew managed to mock him. Most of his relatives and friends, including Gizzio and Matthew Ripa, refused to even see him.

Cardinal Pignatelli, however, greeted him with kindness. After listening sympathetically to the details of the preceding six months of anguish, the cardinal voiced an opinion that Alphonsus frankly did not expect to hear. "It will not do to abandon Scala for the present," he announced. "Let us turn to God and He will reveal his will to us. Go on with your work. Put your trust in God and pay no heed to men—Heaven will help you."[20]

A fresh breeze was finally blowing toward the future; Cardinal Pignatelli made certain that his opinions became public knowledge in Naples. Two men showed special interest in the encouragement offered by Pignatelli's views: Cesare Sportelli and Januarius Sarnelli.

Cesare Sportelli had been one of the first to offer himself to the service of the Institute, but affairs had detained him in Naples. Now he renewed his intention of following Alphonsus in spite of the opposition the work seemed destined to encounter. For several years after finally joining the Institute, the accomplished lawyer would serve as a catechist until his studies for the priesthood could be completed.

Januarius Sarnelli was the first son of the baron of Ciorani. His life paralleled that of Alphonsus in many ways, for he, too, had attained stature in the legal profession, and he had turned his back on the courts and prepared for the priesthood. Januarius first met Alphonsus at the Chinese College and again as a colleague in the Propaganda. His one desire since his ordination a year before was to help as many as possible to return to God. Alphonsus was a priest he admired and his intention of working for abandoned souls struck a chord in Sarnelli's heart. Following the suggestion of Father Manulio, the Jesuit whose wisdom Alphonsus himself admired, Sarnelli accompanied the missionary and Peter Romano on a mission given at Ravello.

Sarnelli returned to Naples convinced of his vocation. But the story of Sister Maria Celeste's exile had just reached the city and aroused a new storm of controversy. On July 2, Sarnelli warned Alphonsus:

> People here are saying that the Institute was based on the revelations of a fanatical visionary and now is in ruins; that if you do not abandon the enterprise you will be left alone on the rocks of Scala; and that if the bishop still tolerates you, it is not because you are a member of the Institute but because you are Alphonsus Liguori. They have gone so far as to say that the Propaganda ordered me to leave the mission at Ravello and return to Naples.
>
> It is a positive blessing that I have been obliged to come back here, for I shall be able to remove the prejudice of our friends and foil the malice of our enemies. Heavens! what an uproar they will make when they learn of my resolution.[21]

Sarnelli's determination rekindled the desires of his close friend, Mazzini. The young priest had been frustrated for several months, always hoping to join Alphonsus and always being told by his director to wait a little longer. When Falcoia was told of the circumstances, his solution was simple: "When wise and prudent men have no doubt about Mazzini's vocation, why not follow their advice in spite of the objections of his director? We must obey God rather than a man whose commands are, after all, only binding by reason of their conformity with the divine will."[22] Mazzini chose to wait as he was directed, and a year later he was allowed to join the Institute.

Peace came to Scala at last. The new members desired only to help each other to love God even more than they had in the past. As they chanted the Office together and shared in the cooking experiments of Brother Curtius, they experienced the joy of serving a God of love. Alphonsus discovered a beautiful cave not far from the monastery, and would sometimes wander to this spot on the mountain to study or to pray. Whenever he would later find himself at Scala, he would visit the cave he called his "beloved grotto," and recall memories of these happy days.

By autumn the group was involved in intense missionary activity in a number of villages along the Amalfi coast. Everywhere they went they were welcomed by the peasants as poor men who loved Jesus Christ. When news of their success reached Naples, the voices of ridicule had to turn to other subjects.

Several young priests, having witnessed the zeal of the new missionaries, expressed an interest in their work. But many of those Alphonsus considered suited to the apostolate to which they had pledged themselves never arrived at the new novitiate at Schiavi. Even those who managed to survive all the obstacles culture and fate had devised left one by one until Alphonsus found himself with no novices at all. It had been estimated that Naples alone supported over 81,000 priests at the moment. Alphonsus was trying so desperately to increase the size of his young community. What made his task so difficult?

Three factors seem to occur regularly enough to be considered the principle causes of the difficulty. 1) The number of priests living in Naples is misleading. Many of them lived with their families and were not actually engaged in any apostolate at all. Their only obligation was to celebrate Mass regularly in a specified chapel, and stipends guaranteed them a reasonable income.[23]

2) Very few priests continued their studies in order to prepare for receiving the faculties necessary to administer the sacrament of Penance. While many of these priests led comfortable lives in proximity to great poverty, not all of them were guilty of the abuses that have been attacked by historians surveying the state of the Neopolitan clergy of his century.[24] But it is apparent even from the complaints of Alphonsus himself, that 3) it was very difficult to convince such priests that their vocation might demand leaving such a comfortable existence in order to embrace a life of uncertainty and poverty in an attempt to glean at least a few souls for God in some remote mountain village.

The Marquis asked Fiorillo to have Alphonsus draw up for him a brief summary of the history and the rule of the Congregation. Alphonsus willingly complied with the request and immediately sent one of the most concise explanations of the scope and origin of the Congregation ever written. It is interesting to note that no mention is made of how many priests are involved.

January, 1736

Four years have passed since a number of priests formed themselves into an association in the town of Scala. Subsequently at the request of Msgr. Vilante, Bishop of Cajazzo, they founded another at Ciorani in the diocese of Salerno. They have fully satisfied the bishops who have asked for their services, the people among whom they live, and the neighboring districts where their preaching has produced a marked improvement in the morals of the inhabitants.

Their principal aim is to imitate as closely as possible, with the help of divine grace, the life and virtues of Our Lord Jesus Christ. In this they set before themselves their own spiritual advantage and that of the people of the kingdom—especially the most forsaken of those to whom they render spiritual aid. In their houses they lead a community life under obedience to their Superior, and perform the functions of the sacred ministry, such as instruction, confessions, the superintendence of schools, confraternities, and other devout gatherings.

They go about the dioceses in which they are established giving missions and, as a means of preserving the good results which they have been enabled by the grace of God to effect, they return from time to time to the districts which have been evangelized to hear confessions and to confirm the people in their good resolutions by another series of instructions and sermons, and by their spiritual advice.

In the monastery as well as abroad they try, with the help of divine grace, to follow closely in the footsteps of the Most Holy Redeemer, Jesus Crucified, so that they might teach the people by example as well as by precept.

As a means of attaining this end, there are twelve points of rule set forth in their constitutions. The headings of these are: Faith, Hope, Love of God, Charity among themselves, Poverty, Purity of Heart, Obedience, Humility of Heart, Mortification, Recollection, Prayer, Self-abnegation and Love of the Cross.

Each of the members spends one day of each week in retreat so that he might be able to work with more ardor afterwards in seeking the spiritual welfare of his neighbor. In their houses they consecrate a large portion of each day to silence, recollection, choir, mortification and to meditation, which is practiced three times a day—in the morning before Office, in the afternoon about Vesper time, and in the evening after Compline. The examination of conscience is made in the morning before dinner and in the evening before they retire to rest. They hold conferences at home in which they consider questions of theology, spirituality, and techniques useful for helping the neglected population.

Their houses are to contain only a few subjects. As for their sustenance, they try not to be a burden on anyone; they live on their families' resources which they have handed over to their superiors, and on such offerings as may be made spontaneously for the love of Jesus Christ by the faithful.

Such in substance is a short compendium of the rules of the Institute of the Most Holy Savior.[25]

The Marquis was impressed with the document that Alphonsus submitted to him and promised to use his influence on behalf of the struggling Congregation. Only one man now stood between Alphonsus and the royal approbation he needed: Bernard Tannuci, Minister of Justice to Don Carlos.

Who was this man who wielded so much power? Austin Berthe, the famous French biographer of Saint Alphonsus, quoted earlier authors who speak of Tannuci as "one of the evil influences of the eighteenth century."[26] Tannuci, according to them, was "a friend to the king but not to the country, a zealous defender of princely omnipotence understood by the pedantic irreligiousness of the time, animated by a proud and despotic spirit which paid no heed either to history or the national character. Tannuci gradually reduced the Church to a condition of servitude, Berthe charges, "ruined its influence with the people, and thus prepared the way for the catastrophe in which the eighteenth century closed."[27]

Emperor Joseph of Austria saw Tannuci in a little different light in 1769 even if Austria had recently lost a very valuable kingdom; he wrote:

Good morals and disinterestedness are attributed to Tannuci. He accepts no favors, but his wife does; he is a good worker; being all-powerful, he must do everything, and being jealous of his authority, every trifle must pass through his hands. He is a Tartuffe, outwardly humble and punctilious in unimportant matters that might raise comment but otherwise a scoundrel...He only thinks of himself and turns all means lawful and unlawful to his personal profit.[28]

A more objective evaluation might be gained from a report of William Hamilton sent to Lord Shelburne in 1767 regarding this man of power.

His honesty is unsuspected and all the world agrees

that he has taken more pains to raise than to enrich himself....He wishes to do well but as he has learned policy from books of law alone, he sees too much with the eyes of a lawyer....He hates monks and priests and does not love the Court of Rome, but instead of taking the true method of setting bounds to the avarice of the clergy and the ambition of the priests, he contents himself with openly mortifying them and showing them the contempt he has for them....The idea of his knowledge renders him obstinate and occasions him doing business with a harshness that, even with a good heart, one contracts by having too good an opinion of oneself.[29]

Croce, who has written a more sympathetic study of Tannuci, portrays him as a hypochondriac who took refuge in work. He paints a picture of a Tannuci who was "truly Tuscan in his hatred of the abstract and love of the concrete. His conception of government was domestic and paternal and he had no sympathy for parliamentary or democratic systems."[30]

Writing to a friend, Tannuci himself mused: "Sovereigns are too mighty to associate with poor little private individuals with mutual pleasure. Pleasure lies in the horizontal: it is uncomfortable always to lift one's head and eyes in conversation with a sovereign. They differ too much from ourselves and that is all as it should be....To the eyes and mind of sovereigns, we private individuals are as flies, butterflies, and sometimes good. We are far more valued by God who came down to live and die in the world than we are by sovereigns."[31]

Whether his actions stemmed from a sincere desire to improve the lot of the population of the kingdom and to enhance the dignity of his prince, or from personal ambition and a vicious desire to destroy the institutional Church (which would not seem to be the case), Tannuci made a special effort to curb the material wealth of the Church of Naples, leveling his sights primarily at a multitude of religious orders.[32] As part of his program, he actively discouraged the formation of *any* new congregation. Needless to say, Alphonsus was forced to forget for a considerable length of time any hope of royal approbation.

By 1736, four years after the foundation of the work, the house at Scala had to be abandoned because of financial difficulties. The house at Villa degli Schiavi had already been closed because of the persecution of a few secular priests who filled the minds of the people with persistent charges of greed and immorality against the few priests of the Most Holy Savior. Only the new foundation at Ciorani, built through the generosity of the Sarnelli family, remained to shelter the Congregation.

Alphonsus, after recovering from a renewed attack of disappointment, realized why God had permitted such apparent misfortune. Writing to Falcoia on July 12, 1737, he reasoned:

God has permitted our latest trials, and I find consolation in the fact that we had become too greatly dispersed. Bitter experience teaches me that when the subjects are few in number, the observance of the rule relaxes, fervor grows cold, perseverance is endangered. I can assure you that all this is worthy of consideration.[33]

Falcoia agreed with Alphonsus immediately. Six months later he confirmed his support: "Birds must return to the nest to gather strength for a safe flight. It is much better to form good missionaries than to preach many sermons with little fruit and what fruit there is gained at the expense of a plant without roots."[34]

The house at Ciorani, built under the supervision of Father Rossi, provided an excellent setting for a retrenchment of community life. Only one wing had been completed, but it contained enough cells for both the professed and the few novices that had joined them. Alphonsus himself chose to convert a small closet under a staircase into his own cell, furnishing it with an undersized bed and a single wooden table.

Father Villani described the Congregation during this period.

We lived in a very poor house and we lived in common under a constitution which was not yet written, but which was observed as strictly as the rule of the most austere orders. Devoted entirely to recollection, the practice of virtue, and to the severest penances, we gave our-

selves up to spiritual reading, meditation, and work with
a holy ardor which the mortified life of our founder still
further increased.[35]

The house at Ciorani, besides providing a haven for the returning missionaries, served as an important retreat center as well,
for both diocesan priests and laymen. Soon the small portion of
the original building that had been temporarily allotted for this
purpose proved inadequate. Everyone agreed that a new wing
should be built. But Father Rossi, practical as always, pointed out
that the funds available for construction amounted to a little more
than two dollars. Alphonsus listened carefully to all the factors
that made building impossible and shook his head. "My dear Father," he said, "we must not operate like businessmen. When they
want to build, they get together the necessary expense money and
only then do they begin the work. We must do just the opposite—
begin the work and then ask Divine Providence to pay the work-
men for us. With your system we will never be able to put one
stone upon another."[36] The foundation for the new wing was
begun, using the capital of the original two dollars, but soon con-
tributions from retreatants and friends of the Congregation enabled the fathers to complete the wing. The financing was not
without peril and not without accusations of greed leveled by a
few disgruntled enemies. But the audacity of the enterprise con-
tradicts those who point to Alphonsus as the ever overcautious
man.

While Alphonsus was trying to draw together the strands
needed to weave a community spirit, his friend, Father Sarnelli,
remained in Naples. For over a year he had suffered from a serious illness that permanently damaged his health, and Alphonsus
feared that the cold of Ciorani would only aggravate his condition.

During the years he remained in the city of Naples, Sarnelli
pursued two very important goals. His first efforts focused on the
problem of prostitution. It was not uncommon to encounter girls
of thirteen or fourteen who had been forced to sell themselves to
strangers in order to put a little cheap food on the family table.
Thousands of young women, forced by necessity rather than choice

into a life without hope, turned from God in shame and despair. The city had written them off as worthless and did little either to discourage them or to help them.

Before entering the Congregation, Sarnelli had begun to work on a pamphlet stressing the necessity of government action to combat the situation. Alphonsus had encouraged him to finish it and he did, giving it the weighty title: "Reasons Catholic, Legal and Political, Which Oblige the Civil Power to Protect a City Against the Ravages of Public Immorality."[37] During his stay in Naples, Sarnelli resolved to distribute the pamphlet and publicly demand enforcement of the steps it outlined.

To the surprise of almost everybody *but* Sarnelli, a royal ordinance appeared May 4, 1758, declaring that prostitution was illegal and would be abolished. Bernard Tannuci, who was proving such a cross to the community at Ciorani, became the champion of Sarnelli's crusade. On May 14, 1758, police raided every known house of prostitution in Naples. Private homes, hotels, and rooming houses were closed and their tenants evicted.

Houses of refuge were opened to provide food and shelter for those who were suddenly homeless. Sarnelli himself was instrumental in obtaining dowries for those who still found an opportunity for marriage. Those who were unwilling to begin a new life found it easier to find a new city in which to carry on their trade.

Surveying what had been accomplished, Sarnelli once again took up his pen and directed his efforts this time to comment on the success of the combined efforts of Church and State. "Let those nearsighted politicians blush who were not content with merely opposing the campaign but declared that it could not succeed. Let them know that the arm of God is not shortened and that He lends His aid to difficult enterprises undertaken for his glory. As for human justice, it attains its ends easily provided it is resolved to do so."[38]

Fortified by the apparent success of the citywide campaign against prostitution, Sarnelli turned to the second stage of his plan to transform Naples. Like Alphonsus, he believed that prayer is *the* great means of salvation, and following the pattern that seemed so effective in his first crusade, Sarnelli wrote a work entitled *The World Sanctified by Mental Prayer.*[39] After tracing the importance of mental prayer in forming a truly Christian community from the time of the Apostles to the Renaissance, he described the effects of the determination of Saint Charles Borromeo to reestablish it throughout the diocese of Milan. Finally, he used every argument he could find to encourage every priest in Naples to teach his people how to pray. The work concluded with several sample meditations that might be used. The dedication to the book captures the spirit of confidence and hope with which Sarnelli appealed to Cardinal Spinelli, Archbishop of Naples.

Your Eminence will protect this movement, based as it is on the infallible authority of the Scriptures, warmly recommended by the Fathers and Councils of the Church and the Apostolic Constitutions. Your excellent parish priests and missionaries will accept with respect your salutary ordinances on the subject. What a glory it would be for your Eminence to follow the notable example set by Saint Charles who by means of common prayer reformed the morals of an entire people, uprooted innumerable abuses, restored discipline, and made a true sanctuary of his diocese.[40]

In hopes of reaching more people by means of the printed word than he ever could in person, Sarnelli sent a complimentary copy to every bishop in Italy. Afterwards, however, he thought of several questions, and sent a series of five letters to each bishop, further explaining various points of his argument.

Cardinal Spinelli was more than willing to cooperate with Sarnelli in promoting mental prayer, and both agreed that the most practical way to approach the crusade was to launch a mission in every part of the diocese coordinating the efforts of the priests and stressing the role of mental prayer in leading a truly Christian life. The next step was convincing Alphonsus Liguori that he was the only man who could lead such an effort. Writing to Alphonsus on February 18, 1741, he pleaded: "Come you must, and you may be certain that your success will surpass even your desires."[41]

After weighing the situation at Ciorani, Alphonsus decided to decline the offer and even journeyed to Naples to present his reasons for doing so to Cardinal Spinelli personally. All of the priests residing at Ciorani were in poor health, except Father Villani, partially due to the poor climate and partially due to sheer overwork. Consequently, Alphonsus did not feel he could leave the community for the great length of time such a mission would require. Cardinal Spinelli listened to all of his very valid arguments and replied firmly: "I am your Superior and wish to be obeyed." Alphonsus bowed to the dictates of obedience and began organizing a mission band, drawing heavily on his former colleagues of the Propaganda.

After carefully instructing each of the missionaries in the procedure to be followed, Alphonsus plunged into the work at hand. Without pausing for rest, he gave extensive missions in Bari, San Sebastino, Bosco, San Giorgio, Resina, San Giovani, Ponticelli, and Polleca. No village was too small as the missionaries carried their message of the importance of establishing a regular program of mental prayer to everyone who would listen.

Alphonsus was seldom hailed as a famous missionary or a "saint on earth" when he first appeared in a village. Riding a fleabitten donkey and wearing an obviously patched cassock that sagged from his shoulders like a thin tent, he was often mistaken for a beggar or a servant of one of the priests with whom he traveled. The story is told of the peasant who turned to one of his friends at the conclusion of the first sermon of one of the missions and whispered: "If the cook preaches so well, what must the others be like!"[42]

After working for a solid year without relief, Alphonsus felt compelled to answer the urgent pleas of Falcoia and the community at Ciorani, and asked to be relieved of his role in the great mission. The cardinal at first refused to listen to any such proposal but after persistent requests, bowed to the request. He demanded, however, that if Alphonsus was to leave, Sarnelli must assume leadership of the project. This Sarnelli agreed to do although his already failing health was very near the final breaking point.

By the end of the mission, a year after Alphonsus returned to Ciorani, the diocese of Naples was the talk of Italy. Prayer had become so much a part of the daily life of some villages that a bell in the square called all of the inhabitants to prayer at appointed times of the day. There is no question that the work had a profound effect on the spiritual life of Naples, although it was not to last as long as either Sarnelli or Alphonsus hoped. The original book of Sarnelli's that had sparked the ambitious undertaking reached the hands of the pope himself, and he issued a decree strongly advising every bishop to stress the value of prayer among the common people and urging them to make use of missions in accomplishing this goal.

The results of the crusade helped Alphonsus to realize more than before the value of the printed word.

By the time Alphonsus reached Ciorani, word arrived that Falcoia was dying. For several years the aging bishop had been in ill health and the burden of his office weighed heavily on the little strength he could muster. Father Sportelli functioned for some months as his confidential secretary, relieving him of many of the burdens of his work and even carrying on the correspondence he dictated, since a serious stroke made it impossible for Falcoia to write more than a single sentence at a time. Violent headaches added to his suffering.

Writing to Father Villani on March 25, Sportelli reported:

> Yesterday our hearts were broken when Monsignor blessed us and promised us he would remember us forever. He burst into tears—the first time I had ever seen him weep—and then said: "Love Jesus Christ with your whole hearts, love Him in truth and not only in words."[43]

On April 20, 1743, Monsignor Falcoia died peacefully at the age of eighty. His eyes were fixed on a picture of Mary.

CHAPTER 5

General of
"An Army of Beggars"

The death of Falcoia forced Alphonsus to stand back and take a good look at the state of the Institute. In the absence of both royal and papal approbation, it was simply a group of secular priests working for a common goal. A definite superior general had never been elected and the constitutions had not yet been given final form.

A month after Falcoia's death, Alphonsus called a chapter to elect a rector major. Seven members composed the chapter: Alphonsus, Sportelli, Mazzini, Rossi and Villani, and Paul Cafaro and Benignum Giordano, who had joined the group after the great mission in Naples. Father Sportelli was elected president of the chapter, and Alphonsus hoped that this was an indication of his possible election as rector major. Three ballots, however, failed to give any member the necessary two-thirds majority.

Sportelli, consequently, suggested that the session adjourn to allow each member to pray earnestly for openness to the will of God. When the second session convened, Alphonsus received every vote but his own.[1]

Alphonsus, the new rector major, elected for a life term, chose as his new spiritual director Paul Cafaro, one of the newest members of the Congregation, and vowed obedience to his advice, as he had earlier to both Father Pagano and Monsignor Falcoia.

At the close of the chapter, Alphonsus directed three of the seven fathers, under the leadership of Sportelli, to found a new house at Nocera de Pagani, twenty-five miles from Naples. Don Francis Contoldi had offered Alphonsus his entire estate and a yearly income to support the foundation, and the bishop and clergy of the diocese had earnestly asked that he consider the proposal.

Fathers Sportelli, Mazzini, Giordano and Brothers Vitus Curtius and Francis Tartiglione arrived at Pagani and temporarily took up residence in a private home until the completion of a monastery. Difficulties, as always, stood in the way of the project. A royal decree of April 9, 1740, sent to all the governors of the province, decreed:

> No one may permit the erection of a monastery or church without the formal authorization of the King; and in case of contravention of this order, they shall enjoin the suspension of the works, and after giving notice of the fact at the royal audience, await the decision of his Majesty.[2]

The formal petition for permission to build the monastery had already been forwarded to the king, but many people in Pagani predicted that it would never be granted. Alphonsus refused to waiver. While waiting for word from Naples, the fathers gave a number of missions in the area, helping to win the good will and support of the people among whom they hoped to work.

Finally, on April 10, 1743, the answer to the petition arrived in the form of a formal decree stating in part: "A work so excellent and holy as that of winning neglected souls to God has met with the complete approval of his Majesty."[3] The first stone of the church was laid on July 22, 1743, and the monastery was built with the help of many of the townspeople, following a plan drawn up by the architect Comafonte.

Alphonsus was sure that the Congregation had finally reached a firm footing. Ten postulants, the majority of them already ordained priests, had asked to be admitted to the novitiate at Ciorani during the missions that had been conducted in the area surrounding Pagani. Such a large number of novices necessitated appointing a novice master, and Alphonsus again chose Paul Cafaro, his own spiritual director, for this task.

In order to help the novices deepen their lives of prayer, Alphonsus wrote his first published work, *Visits to the Most Blessed Sacrament,* and in the preface to the first edition, explains what prompted him to publish the work.

> Some of the meditations which you are about to read were intended to help the young men of our Congregation in the daily visit which they make, according to custom, to the most Holy Sacrament; but a devout layman, hearing them read during a retreat in our house, wanted them printed at his own expense.[4]

Several sources suggest that the layman was probably Don Joseph, the father of Alphonsus.

The triumph of Alphonsus should have been complete; but the month of June brought word that his dear friend, Father Sarnelli, was on his deathbed. For two years he had been engaged in mission after mission at Naples, burning with the desire to teach the whole world how to pray. Threat of the plague had hung over Naples for several months after the close of the crusade, and Sarnelli had made every effort to ease the sufferings of those who were forced into drafty buildings to die without pity. Dragging himself from hospital to hospital, he stopped only long enough to do what he seemed to do best: write. Several short works survived this period, including those on how to combat the plague, charity toward the dead, on the duties of priests, and finally the comprehensive outline for a work on devotion to the Blessed Virgin.[5]

Writing to Sister Mary Angela at Scala, Sarnelli admitted: "I do not know whether I am on earth or in purgatory—I feel rather as if I were in hell."[6] Finally, on June 30, he said to the brothers Alphonsus had sent to assist him: "Get out my most worn clothes to bury me in so that nothing may be lost on my account."[7] Alphonsus carried grief over the loss of Sarnelli far into his old age.

After Sarnelli's death, his portrait was placed in the monastery at Ciorani, bearing the following inscription:

Don Januarius Sarnelli of the Congregation of the Most Holy Savior. A man of eminent holiness and great learning, he distinguished himself by his charity towards the poor and especially towards the sick in the hospitals, and by his ardent zeal for the salvation of souls. Mortified to excess and endowed with invincible patience, he had to suffer much for Jesus Christ. At last, laden with merits and good works, he rendered up his soul to God in the year of Our Lord 1744, on the 30th day of June, aged forty-two years.[8]

Later, Alphonsus wrote a short biography of Sarnelli, praising his sanctity and expressing the hope that he would one day be called "Saint." Today the Church has declared Father Januarius Sarnelli "Venerable."

Less than six months later, Alphonsus once again set out to expand the influence of the Congregation. While preaching a mission near Ciorani, the governor of Iliceto happened to hear him, and at once praised the missionaries as the key to the fulfillment of one of his greatest desires, a desire that was shared by many of the inhabitants of Iliceto. After speaking to Alphonsus on the subject of a possible foundation in his town, Calvini, the governor of Iliceto, promptly wrote to Canon Casti.

The Fathers of St. Saviour seem to me to be the very men for the object you have in mind. (I would willingly bequeath my property, he said, to a religious order which would establish itself in the Church of Our Lady of Consolation, to receive the pilgrims and evangelize the towns and villages of Apulia.) I see them at work here; they do not seek their own interests but the salvation of souls. At their head is the Cavaliere Alphonso de Liguori....Everything leads me to believe they would accept a foundation at Iliceto where they would be well situated for the exercise of their special ministry, which is to help carry help to the neglected peasants of the country side.[9]

Alphonsus, with Paul Cafaro and two other companions,

stopped at Iliceto to survey the situation on the way to Modugno, where they were scheduled to give a mission.

Climbing the hill to the sagging hermitage of Our Lady of Consolation, Alphonsus reacted both as an artist and as a missionary. The thick green forest of the fertile slopes and the two springs near the house itself touched the artistic string of his temperament. The missionary in him responded even more strongly to the fresh realization of how poor the thousands of nomadic shepherds and goatherds were who wandered down from the mountains every winter to allow their flocks to graze on the floor of the valley below him. And how little provision had been made for their welfare. Had not his Congregation pledged itself to serve the poor? What was God revealing to them?

After serious deliberation Alphonsus consented. Canon Casti, as he had promised, donated the property to the fathers of the Most Holy Savior on December 19, 1744, with the provision that ownership of the land and properties would not change hands until his death. Writing to Rossi, Alphonsus enthusiastically described the advantages of Our Lady of Consolation.

> The property we have received consists of over 700 acres of arable land, of a vineyard, and of some houses with an olive plantation. The country is fertile and produces everything: wood, grain, vegetables, good wine, excellent cheese, and goats, and a certain kind of cheese, the like of which I have not tasted before...and a fish pond by which we can water the garden at all times and keep it green.[10]

For once, it seemed, a foundation would begin with a minimum of difficulty. After all, they had many promises of financial support, a building of sorts to begin with, and judging from the impressions of the agricultural potential of the area, starvation was indeed a remote prospect. And yet, in the same letter to Rossi, Alphonsus penned a sentence that would prove to be prophetic: "Let us keep our spirits. We shall be beggars all our lives."[11]

The poverty of the nomadic shepherds he longed to serve was greater than he had realized. Writing to Father Sportelli on December 28, 1744, Alphonsus partially described the conditions under which they hoped to work: "There are ninety thousand abandoned souls but, O God, how abandoned! Here the good that we can do under the circumstances in which we are is immense, different from Nocera and Ciorani. I omit writing all. But when you come, please God, you will see it."[12]

The climate and scenery promised to be so conducive to prayer that Alphonsus decided to transfer the novitiate from Ciorani to Iliceto. Yet, in the midst of such promise, the community was soon forced to a level of poverty as great as that endured by the abandoned souls they served. Many of the promises of financial assistance they had received turned out to be just that: promises. The actual ownership of the property on which they lived, having been granted under the terms of an *inter vivos* trust, would not actually become theirs until the death of the donor. Undoubtedly, when Alphonsus had surveyed the wealth of possibilities the land offered in the way of food for the community table, he had overlooked an important consideration. The fathers had taken possession of the land in the middle of winter! The fields had not been cultivated in the preceding season and it would be many months until a possible harvest. Several times in his life Alphonsus would insist that he was not a businessman. This oversight certainly proved it.

The archaic building that now housed the novices as well as the fathers was in need of major repairs, and winter winds forced snow through gaping cracks in the walls and roof, spreading it over floors, furniture, and even beds. Alphonsus, concerned with the welfare of his community, but unable to change conditions, begged them: "My dear Fathers and Brothers, we are indeed living very miserably; but after all, what have we come to this mountain for if not to suffer for the love of Jesus Christ?"[13]

In desperation Alphonsus wrote to Andrew Calvino, who had first extended the offer of financial support, and told him frankly:

> ...if God does not come to our assistance I shall be obliged to dismiss my companions so as not to see them die of hunger. We eat only beans and drink only water, yet I am already sixty ducats in debt.[14]

At the end of several months of living under the same conditions, it was manifestly apparent to everyone that something had to be done. Alphonsus pleaded: "Have patience for just a little longer." On February 3, 1746, Canon Casti died in the arms of Alphonsus. A few days later the congregation received actual ownership of the property and a revenue of about 300 ducats a year. The bequest was never enough to lift the foundation from a level of subsistence, but it seemed like a miracle to those who had struggled for so long on infinitely less.

Most people would hesitate to even consider another foundation after experiencing hardships necessitated by this undertaking. But while the community at Iliceto was still hovering on the brink of financial disaster, the Archbishop of Conza, Joseph de Nicolo, offered Alphonsus a church dedicated to the Blessed Virgin in the small town of Caposele. While it seemed unlikely that he would accept the offer, Alphonsus agreed to at least visit the town. With Fathers Villani, Genovese, and Garzelli, he departed on May 22, 1746 for Caposele. At least this time he was sure that he was seeing the surroundings in spring weather!

Although suffering from severe neuralgia, he went on foot to survey the church of Mater Domini. The moment he saw it at the top of the hill, he was reminded of Our Lady of Consolation at Iliceto. Unexpectedly, after praying for the light to know the will of God, he agreed to accept the foundation if he was provided with means for its support.

The experience at Iliceto taught Alphonsus at least one thing, however, and he asked the archbishop for a guaranteed annual income of 500 ducats. The archbishop hesitated at first but finally gave in to the persistent pleas of his advisors. He agreed to the terms as soon as the fathers obtained royal permission to build.

Sportelli, the seasoned pioneer of the Congregation, was immediately appointed to begin the foundation and Father Garzelli and Brother Gaspar Corvino soon joined him.

In spite of the apparent caution of Alphonsus, the tiny community suffered a stormy first year of existence. Father Garzelli describes conditions in the new house.

Our household effects were limited to three mattresses and one change of linen. We had to cover our beds with cloaks instead of blankets. We had only one knife and fork among the three of us, but I managed to make two wooden forks for the brother and myself. We made known our poverty to the sisters of Solofra and they gave us three blankets and knives and forks, only asking for the wooden forks in return. More than once we were obliged to beg a little bread and were very glad to get it.[15]

The building of the house consumed the energies of the ailing Sportelli and, near exhaustion, he confessed to Alphonsus: "Only God knows the difficulties and pain this house of Caposele is costing me. I am often tempted to fly to the desert or to become a Trappist."[16] Pastoral duties eroded what little strength he had left.

In midwinter 1748, less than two years after the building of the foundation at Caposele, Sportelli traveled to Ciorani to preach a retreat. Before he could reach his destination, he was caught in a heavy snowstorm. Worn out and burning with a high fever, he collapsed in the middle of the road and discovered that a stroke had paralyzed one side of his body. He found it almost impossible to continue in the bitter cold, but somehow he managed to reach Ciorani. His career as an active missionary was over; the restless pioneer now faced life as a permanent invalid.

Alphonsus, meanwhile, was sharing the lot of the novices at Iliceto. Three more novices had arrived in October, among them Antony Tannoia who was later to write the first biography of his superior: *The Life and Institute of the Venerable Alfonso Maria Liguori*.[17] In order to help these novices become the missionaries they desired to be, Alphonsus had already published his *Visits*. Now he somehow found time to write *Meditations on the Passion* for their use in their evening meditation, although the work did not appear in print at this time. Knowing, too, that after their novitiate they would have to become proficient in the field of moral theology if they hoped to become holy confessors, the weary missionary began the most comprehensive work of his career, his *Moral Theology*,[18] which would take decades to complete.

Even his brush was called into service as he painted a large scene of the Adoration of the Shepherds, used as a setting for the novitiate crib, a scene that was particularly meaningful at Iliceto. The poverty that had existed originally at Iliceto was once more a pressing problem as an increase of novices added to the community table. Father Garzelli vividly describes conditions as they existed.

We used to eat bread black as coal made of rye mixed with flour and bran, and often even that was not to be had....Meat we never saw. At most the soup contained a little lard, or a piece of an ox which had died of exhaustion. On such days as those we thought that we were having a banquet....Our shirts had been so often repaired that the original material had completely disappeared.... Our habits were made of odd pieces of old cloth. Bits of rags served as our handkerchiefs. Our blankets were almost transparent. As for the house, it was colder indoors than out, for the wind blew through the holes in the dilapidated walls. Our windows were filled not with glass but with an oiled paper which let in daily a little light. I stop here, for if I were to tell all, people would refuse to believe me.[19]

Several novices, after enduring the bitter fruits of poverty for several months, gave up and left Iliceto. Alphonsus had tried in vain to provide somehow a better living for the community, but his pockets contained only holes.

Finally, on February 5, 1747, Alphonsus sent the novices back to Ciorani and soon followed them himself. Father Paul Cafaro was appointed rector of Iliceto and remained behind with a few courageous companions.

While storms had been raging at both Iliceto and Caposele, Ciorani had remained a comparative sea of calm. Father Rossi, as always, had been spending his spare time trying to complete construction, and the missionaries had met with success in several surrounding districts. By the end of the year six new postulants arrived, as if to replace those who could not endure the poverty at Iliceto.

The missionaries had accomplished a great deal. Four houses continued to exist, and vocations to the Institute were steadily increasing, but Alphonsus was still deeply troubled. In the eyes of the king and the pope, the members of the Congregation of the Most Holy Saviour were still nothing more than a group of secular priests. The time had come to work seriously for approbation if the Congregation was to remain in existence.

With a heavy heart Alphonsus set out for Naples with Brother Tartiglione. After several weeks of conferences with friends of the Congregation, Alphonsus finally gained an audience with the king. Stressing the need for the special apostolate to which the Institute was dedicated, Alphonsus made every effort to win the king's favor. While apparently encouraging him, the king had refused to give an answer and referred the matter to the Grand Almoner and the Council of Ministers.

The case dragged on and the desperation of Alphonsus became more apparent. Writing to Mazzini, he asked: "Pray now to Jesus Christ that He may give me strength and light, for I have lost sleep, appetite, etc. Yesterday morning the Grand Almoner at the beginning seemed to shut us out completely. Then the affair came up for discussion again. Tomorrow I have to begin all over again."[20]

Father de Robertis, who traveled from Ciorani, watched him go painfully from door to door, exhausted from lack of sleep, always trying to gain support for his cause. On one particularly disheartening day, de Robertis reports, three former acquaintances literally slammed their doors in his face.[21] In a letter of August, 1747, Alphonsus poured out part of the frustration that was building in his heart.

Continue to pray for the Congregation and for me, who am broken in two in Naples dealing with these Ministers who have made me weary of life. I have a bucket of poison in my heart; I can do no more; I should like to escape, and yet I cannot escape from Naples. It is imperative that I help to get the cause voted at the present time, as quickly as possible.[22]

Alphonsus soon received word from the king, but not on the petition concerning approbation for the Institute. Instead, the king announced that he had decided to appoint Alphonsus bishop of Palermo! Alphonsus pleaded, begged, and declared that he had vowed never to accept such a post. The king only waved away his objection as further proof of his suitability for the office. Pleading with every influential friend he could contact in Naples, Alphonsus begged them to help convince the king that his removal at this crucial moment meant certain ruin for his beloved Congregation. Finally, Marquis Brancone persuaded the king to withdraw the offer.

At long last the Grand Almoner recommended that the Council of Ministers approve the Congregation but added a number of deadly restrictions to his consent.

1) The new society was to receive into its ranks the missionaries of the Blessed Sacrament (founded by Mannarini at the time of the first break in which Tosquez had been so instrumental. Mannarini had petitioned the king to unite the two Congregations—Alphonsus had refused to consider the move on several occasions).

2) The missionaries were not permitted to establish themselves in any other part of the kingdom without the permission of the king.

3) They should not have for any house more than a maximum revenue of a thousand ducats.[23]

The Council of Ministers, however, vetoed the recommendation on August 25.

Alphonsus was crushed by the news but he refused to despair. Placing his trust in the will of God, he continued to seek support for a new petition. During the agonizing periods of waiting for others to make up their minds, he spent time preaching in a familiar pulpit. He had also managed somehow to give a number of retreats at convents at Naples and preached the novena of the Assumption in the church of St. John.

Six months later, Alphonsus presented a second petition to the king. The prospects for a favorable decision were slim, but he could not resist making every effort to insure the continued existence of the Congregation. During the same period, on the advice of a number of people, he submitted a petition directly to Pope Benedict XIV, asking for papal approbation of the Congregation.[24] While waiting for replies to both petitions, Alphonsus worked in every area of Naples. Even a severe attack of asthma did not prevent him from preaching everywhere. He even conducted a special retreat for the officers and enlisted men of the Naples garrison. A captain, after listening to the first sermon, commented to one of the companions of Alphonsus: "That's a man who goes straight to the point."[25] In spite of the affairs that bound him to Naples, Alphonsus traveled to Ciorani to spend Holy Week with his Institute in silent retreat.

In September of 1748 a skeletal edition of his monumental *Moral Theology* appeared in print, entitled *Annotations to Busenbaum*, and the controversy excited by it undoubtedly had a favorable effect on the Congregation's cause in Rome. Two separate dissertations were appended: one on the doctrine of the Immaculate Conception, and one on the doctrine of infallibility of the pope. Both doctrines were under attack in the eighteenth century and Alphonsus hoped to silence the opposition. In the conclusion to the treatises, he expressed the hope that both would be declared dogmas of the Church.

When he left Naples in August, Alphonsus had failed to receive the approbation of the king, but he had every confidence that he would soon receive word from Rome that the Congregation had won the approval of the Church.

On October 11, he received word that an inquiry would be opened in Rome to consider his petition, and Alphonsus chose Father Villani to represent the Congregation in this very important matter. Taking with him Brother Tartiglione, Villani departed at the end of October with very little money but complex plans for economizing. Reporting to the rector major on November 9, he insisted: "Pray hard for me Father, for all I am fit for is to spoil everything."[26]

Every person of position Villani talked to in Rome gave him different directions and suggestions on how to carry out his assignment until the poor priest was reeling with confusion. Writing to Alphonsus, he complained:

O my Father, they do things here quite differently from
everywhere else. You need great prudence and reserve to
survive. O my God, what has become of simplicity and
sincerity? Words, words, more than you want, but as for
deeds—that is a different thing.[27]

The rounds that were made daily by Villani and the weari-
some detail to which he bent his energies are too complicated to
be told here. But finally, Villani received news that the Congregation had been approved. In his joy he simply wrote in large letters at
the top of a sheet of paper: "GLORIA PATRI! THE CONGRE-
GATION IS APPROVED—ORSINI'S SERVANT HAS JUST
BROUGHT ME THE GREAT NEWS!"[28] The moment Alphonsus
opened the letter, he fell to his knees. At long last—the Congregation was approved! The fathers together sang a truly joyous *Te
Deum.*

On February 25 an apostolic letter arrived confirming the approbation of the Institute and rule of the Congregation under the
title of Fathers of the Most Holy Redeemer. (The name had been
changed to avoid confusion with another Congregation with a
similar name. The change was suggested by authorities in Rome.)

Alphonsus knew that papal approbation did not insure the
continued existence of his Congregation. A simple royal decree
drawn up by ministers hostile to the interests of the Institute could
close all four foundations and order the fathers dispersed in a
matter of days. Even while Villani was still in Rome, Alphonsus
insisted that he make every effort to convince the Neopolitan
ambassador to support their cause. In February, 1749, Villani
answered confidently: "Our Lord is not working miracles in our
favor here in Rome to abandon us in Naples."[29] A few days later,
however, his tone altered considerably: "I am afraid that by attempting too much we shall only succeed in creating greater difficulties
for ourselves. Still you may be sure that I am neglecting no means
to insure success, though to tell the truth, I count little on our
insignificant efforts. It is for God to bring us through this affair."[30]

For years Alphonsus awaited the "right moment" to pressure
for complete recognition of the status of the Fathers of the Holy
Redeemer as a religious congregation. The time did not come in his

lifetime. After several years of fruitless negotiations on the matter, Alphonsus candidly revealed to Mother Angiola of the Discalced Carmelites of Capua, whose spiritual support he valued:

> I think and I always say that Our Lord wishes to mortify my pride and that the approbation will not be obtained until after my death. "It is the Lord, let Him do what is good in His sight" (1 Kings 3:18).[31]

What was the problem? It seemed that ministers close to the king, led by Tannuci and Fraggianni, contended that all religious orders, even the poorest, swallowed up property and amassed great wealth at the expense of the poor people they proposed to serve. They, consequently, insisted that the Congregation of Alphonsus, if recognized, would add to the burden of the poor rather than relieve it.

In fact, on May 4, 1752, the superintendent of customs was ordered by the Council of Ministers to conduct an inquiry into the financial state of the Institute. When the Bishop of Bovino, Monsignor Lucci, testified on behalf of the state of destitution suffered by the fathers, he received the following sarcastic reply: "These people are like the Jesuits. They are beginning in poverty but later on nothing will satisfy them."[32] The rest of the inquiry proceeded in a similar vein. The Congregation was granted permission to exist; and for that Alphonsus was grateful, but its existence was precarious for as long as he lived.

Before examining the problems Alphonsus encountered during his last years as an active missionary, it is important to achieve some sort of overall view of the spirit he tried to instill in those around him over the years he was rector major of the Congregation. What did he hope for those he received into the Institute?

Alphonsus expected each of them to become saints, not just reasonably good religious, but saints! This demanded no less than a radical commitment to Christ the Redeemer. The following letter of Alphonsus to all the fathers and brothers of the Congregation says more than any other words could express, both about the importance he placed on the spirit of the Congregation and about the genuine love Alphonsus had for those with whom he shared his desires.

August 8, 1754
Nocera

Live Jesus, Mary, Joseph and Teresa!

I beg all of you, my Brethren in Jesus Christ, before you hear this letter read, to say the *Veni, Creator Spiritus*, and to ask of God the light to understand and put into practice what in the name of Jesus Christ I write to all and to each one in particular.

My Fathers and my Brothers: it is not yet twenty-two years since the beginning of the Congregation and it is five years since it was approved by the Holy Church, so that at this moment it should not only have maintained its first fervor but should moreover have enriched it. Many, it is true, are behaving well but in others, instead of advancement, there is a lack of spirit. What will become of these I know not: for God has called us into the Congregation to become saints.

Poor Congregation if this lack of spirit spreads among us! What will it be fifty years from now? One should have to weep and say, Poor Jesus Christ! If He is not loved by a member of the Congregation, who has received from Him so many special lights, by whom will He be loved? And why have we entered the Congregation, and for what purpose do we remain in it if we are not trying to become saints?

...I am already old and in bad health, and am already drawing near to the day of account. I desire to be of as much service to you as I can; and God knows how much I love each of you, more than my brothers and my mother....We are all miserable creatures and we all commit faults. I am not pained by passing faults but by those that are permanent and by certain weaknesses that do harm to the whole Community.

...I beg each of you to ask of Jesus Christ his holy love....In order to obtain this love, let us strive to have a great love for the Passion of Jesus Christ....It seems to me impossible for one who thinks often of His Passion not to become full of love for Jesus Christ. There is nothing on which we insist in the missions more than this love for the Passion of Jesus Christ.

...I recommend to you also the love of poverty and beg all to take notice that faults against these two virtues—poverty and obedience—are not and cannot be tolerated in the Congregation; for if the practice of these two virtues fails, the spirit of the Congregation is wholly destroyed and at an end.

Lastly, be assured my brethren, that I love each one of you, after God, as my only love on this earth, and I offer for each of you, from this moment, my blood and my life; for you who are young may do much for the glory of God but as for me, who am old and ill and useless, what more service can I render? And, therefore, I beg you—each of you—if he is at a distance, to write to me whenever he has the need and to banish the idea, which the devil has been making use of to disquiet me and others, that he will annoy me by speaking or writing to me. Be sure that the more one shows me this confidence, the more he binds me to him; and remember that where there is question of consoling one of my brethren I leave everything; and God demands this of me in my office more than anything else.

Live Jesus, Mary, Joseph, Saint Francis Xavier and Saint Teresa!

Brother Alfonso Liguori
of the Most Holy Redeemer[33]

Once the decision was made, once the candidate had sincerely resolved to became a saint, Alphonsus pointed out what made it not only possible but necessary: "Attach yourself to the love of Jesus Christ." To novices especially, who were just beginning to understand what their vocation meant, the rector major spoke of the necessity of living one's life only for love.

Nocera
January 28, 1762

To the Novices at Iliceto
My very dear Brethren,

God knows how much I envy you. Had I only had in my youth, like you, the happiness of living in God's house! Yes, I envy you and I tell you to thank God unceasingly for the grace that He has given you.

Attach yourself more and more to the love of Jesus Christ. He that loves Jesus Christ with his whole heart does not fear to lose Him and he is ready to suffer for the love of Him every kind of pain, of contempt, of poverty. I bless you now in the name of the Holy Trinity and especially of Jesus Christ who by His death has merited for you the supreme grace of holy perseverance.

I beg you to love much the Mother of God and to call her to your aid if you wish to sanctify yourselves. Be full of courage, be joyful! Become saints and love Jesus Christ very much for He gave His life and blood for each one of you.

Become saints and pray to God for me, a poor old man, who is near death without having done anything for God. Do you at least who remain here below love Him for me.

I embrace you in the Sacred Heart of Jesus Christ and bless you anew.

Live Jesus, Mary, Joseph and Teresa![34]

What is perhaps the most beautiful letter ever written by Alphonsus to all the fathers and brothers of the Congregation follows the same central theme:

Arienzo
July 29, 1774

My dearest Brethren in Jesus Christ:

The principal thing I recommend to you is the love of Jesus Christ. Very much are we bound to love Him.

For this end He has chosen us from all eternity and

called us into His Congregation, there to love Him and to make others love Him. What greater honor, what greater mark of love could Jesus Christ show us? He has taken us from the world in order to draw us to His love and so that, during the pilgrimage of this life by which we must pass into eternity, we might think of nothing but of pleasing Him and of bringing those crowds of people to love Him who, every year by means of our ministry, abandon sin and put themselves into the grace of God.

If, therefore, God so highly honors us as to choose us to be the instruments of His glory and of bringing others to love Him, how greatly ought we not to thank and love Him! Let others labor to acquire the reputation of men of honor and talent, but let us try to advance every day more and more in the love of Jesus Christ, and to find opportunities of pleasing Him by offering to Him some mortification or some other act that will be acceptable to Him.

And if we wish to attach ourselves always more and more to the Heart of Jesus Christ, let us always put ourselves in the last place. As members of the Congregation, you would show too great an ingratitude to Jesus Christ who shall love Him with reserve, and should neglect to live as strictly united to God as he might.

My Brothers, when death comes, the light of the candle will disclose to us the graces that the Lord has bestowed upon us in keeping us in the beautiful vocation that He has given us.

You already know that the most efficacious means to enable us to bear contradictions is a great love of Jesus Christ, but for this very much prayer is necessary. To love Jesus Christ is the greatest work that we can perform on this earth but it is a work and a gift that we cannot have of ourselves; it must come to us from Him and He is ready to give it to those who ask Him for it, so that if we are lacking it, it is through our own fault and our own negligence that we have it not.

A day will come, as we may well hope, when we shall

see ourselves all united together in that eternal home, never
more to be separated from one another and where we
shall find united with us many hundreds of thousands of
souls who at one time did not love God but who, brought
back to His grace by means of us, will love Him and will
be for all eternity a cause of gladness to ourselves. Should
not this thought alone spur us on to give ourselves completely to the love of Jesus Christ, and to making others
love Him?

I finish but I could go on forever from the desire I
have that I might see you all filled with love for Jesus
Christ, and working for His glory, especially in these un-
happy times in which we see Jesus Christ so little loved in
the world.

Brother Alfonso Maria[35]

The warmth and genuine love of his community expressed in
the preceding letters did not prevent Alphonsus from bluntly reminding the members on many occasions, both individually and
collectively, that their vocation was to be saints, and the alterna-
tive was to surrender the name "Redemptorist!"

Arienzo
September 30, 1770

My dearest Brethren in Jesus Christ:

...Lack of love for poverty would seem to be more
tolerable if our houses had the revenues of the Fathers of
Chartreuse; whereas, it is a miracle of divine Providence
that each one has even bread enough at table. You know
very well the straits in which all our houses are. There is
but little love of obedience, little love of fraternal charity,
and I hear that some go about complaining first of one
and then of another.

Let each look to himself and if anyone is not pleased
with the Congregation and with regular observance let
him, in the name of God, leave. It is of no importance
that we are few in number, for God does not wish that we
should be numerous but that we be good and holy.

As for me, I am at the end of my course. In my decrepit state and bedridden as I am, what can I do? It is for you, my children, to keep up the Congregation and rest assured that if we conduct ourselves well, God will always help us. The poorer, the more despised, the more persecuted we are, the greater will be the good that we shall do and the greater the reward that Jesus Christ will give us in heaven.

I bless you all, one by one, and I pray to God to fill each of you with His holy love.

Brother Alfonso Liguori[36]

"We are all poor," Alphonsus often said, "rectors, ministers, subjects. Do you know what Rector Major means? It means General of an army of beggars."[37] The same genuine humility that prompted this evaluation was reflected in a hundred other ways in the life of Alphonsus. Thousands of pages of testimony gathered in the course of the process for his canonization brought forth countless proofs that he never demanded anything of others he had not first imposed on himself. On one occasion, a member testified, a visitor was expounding on the nobility of the ancient family of Liguori. "The surest thing about the genealogy of the Liguori," he interrupted, "is that they are descended from a cobbler."[38] And he could not resist adding with a smile: "My ancestor was a cobbler and my father was in the galleys." (Don Joseph was Captain of the Royal Galleys.)

Another priest who was still a novice at Iliceto when Alphonsus resided there, tells us:

I have seen him three times a week washing the dishes with the brothers and the novices. He always took the most fatiguing and disagreeable part of the work. When there were any particularly greasy plates to be cleaned, he seized on them often at the risk of scalding his fingers in the boiling water. I remember that once I myself, ashamed to see him at this work, wished to take out of his hands a pot from which he was trying to remove the grease. But he refused to let go. "I am not any better than you," he said, "and what I am you are."...He made his own bed, swept his floor, brushed his shoes, and cleaned his candlestick. His humility led him to wear old patched garments which called forth all kinds of remarks about his appearance.[39]

When those he hoped to see saints did not reveal the same desire, he was quick to spell out what he knew to be the indispensable goal of all those who profess to follow Christ the Redeemer.

To the Fathers and Brothers of the Congregation

Arienzo
June 27, 1773

My dear Brethren and my Children:

I write this time to you with tears in my eyes because I hear that some of you do not live up to the end for which God has called them into our little Congregation, but allow themselves to be carried away by the spirit of pride and disunion.

God does not reign in those hearts in which Christian humility, fraternal charity, and peace do not reign. Our lack of correspondence to the grace of God makes me more afraid than the fiercest persecution.

God wills us to be poor and to be content in poverty, and we ought to thank Him when through His mercy we find a crust of bread on the table, and when we are not in need of that which is strictly necessary. He that is not pleased to live among us poor people, with poor clothes and poor food, may leave the Congregation without troubling us and may go and live at his own home as he pleases, for I am quite ready to give him his dismissal, as God does not wish to have in the house discontented servants who serve Him by force and in continual disturbance.

Let everyone banish from his head that worldly pride of wishing to rival others and to do better than others, and this even in preaching the word of God....We ought to preach, not ourselves indeed, but Christ crucified, His glory and not our own vanity.

I am not afraid even if the greater number leave us. He that remains remains. God has no need of numbers; it is enough if a few good subjects remain. These few will do more good than all the other imperfect, proud, and disobedient subjects.

I conclude, as I began, with tears in my eyes, begging all to conduct themselves well and not to give me any more pain during those few days of life that are before me, and this I hope from the love and obedience that you have always shown me. I bless you all.

Brother Alfonso Maria
of the Most Holy Redeemer[40]

CHAPTER 6

Bishop of the Poor

Alphonsus was sixty-five years old and had outlived all the friends who shared the burdens of the early struggles of the Institute. His days as an active missionary were over, and he had retired to the relative seclusion of the monastery at Pagani to spend the few days left on this earth in prayer and study.

His eyesight, which was wretched, had weakened to the point of semi-blindness, making research a slow and painful process. Partial deafness made it difficult for him to understand rapid conversation unless someone was speaking to him directly. In addition, a severely damaged nerve in his leg[1] had left him with a permanent and pronounced limp, and attacks of asthma frequently reduced him to helplessness. Everything seemed to indicate that God willed the end of his active ministry.

While Father Joseph Paravento was speaking to him around five o'clock on March 9, 1762, a visitor arrived to shatter any hopes Alphonsus might have had for a few years of peaceful seclusion. Monsignor Joseph Locatelli, Apostolic Nuncio, appeared before the aged missionary and after bowing deeply presented himself as "Your Most Illustrious Lordship's servant." Alphonsus was speechless. "The Pope has appointed you Bishop of St. Agata of the Goths," the Nuncio explained. Alphonsus could not believe it; someone was surely playing a joke on an old man! But when the Nuncio's messenger later brought the official letter of appointment, he read his projected fate with tears in his eyes.[2]

Members of the Congregation were unable to console him

during the deep depression that followed. His only hope rested in considering the possibility that the appointment might be simply an indication of the pope's respect for the work of the Congregation. Surely the pope was unaware of his physical condition, thought Alphonsus, and, he composed an answer to the letter of appointment stating what he felt were serious impediments to acceptance of the honor that was offered.[3] If his advanced age and deteriorating health were not reasons enough to exclude him from consideration for the see, surely the pope would understand that he had bound himself by vow to decline any such position. When he finished the letter he handed it resolutely to the Nuncio's messenger and declared: "If I were to see you again, it would kill me."[4]

The following afternoon a letter arrived from Cardinal Spinelli, Archbishop of Naples, disclosing a few of the circumstances that had led him to the decision to appoint him to the diocese of St. Agata.[5] No less than sixty men had formally applied for consideration upon the death of the former bishop and most of them were urgently attempting to "pull strings" to insure their own appointments. After sifting the qualifications of each candidate, it became obvious that none of them really deserved the office to which they aspired. The only solution seemed to involve appointing a man of such obvious sincerity and merit that those who clamored for honor would be shamed into silence. Cardinal Spinelli himself had suggested Don Alphonsus Liguori and Pope Clement XIII had agreed.

Spinelli had tried to soften the blow by pointing out that he could always retire within a reasonable length of time if he found the office too much of a burden for his waning strength. But the cardinal's letter failed to alter the reticence of Alphonsus. "If God does not grant my petition," he swiftly replied, "I will know that he is punishing me for my sins."[6] For ten days he intensified his life of prayer and penance, and struggled with a rising tide of depression. Yet he could never avoid ending even his most urgent petitions for release with the words that had shaped his life: "My God, Your will be done."

Early in the evening of March 19, the Nuncio's messenger arrived with two letters that would confirm his worst fears. Fa-

ther Paravento tells us: "I met with him in the corridor of the
monastery and when I asked him where he was going he answered:
'To Don Alphonsus. His renunciation has not been accepted. I am
bringing letters from the Pope!' I tried to stop him because our
Father had stated several times that the mere sight of the man
would kill him. I told Father Mazzini what the messenger had
told me. Together with Father Cimino, he read the letters and
then both of them went to the cell of Alphonsus."

It was Mazzini who stated the formal decision of the Holy
Father confirming his nomination to the see of St. Agata. "Where
are the letters?" he asked. "Maybe there is some way of interpret-
ing them." But the formal letters left no loopholes and no question of escape.

Most Reverend Father:

I have explained in detail the reasons you have presented for declining your nomination to the episcopate.
His Holiness has expressed admiration for your religious
attachment to the Congregation you have founded and
by your concern for such an apostolic work. Neverthe-
less, his Holiness, knowing the great needs of the Church
of St. Agata, has not, after mature deliberation, thought it
well to change his resolution.

Consequently, by his order, I have to express to you
His will; namely, that without further excuses, you unre-
servedly accept functions that will permit your zeal to be
exercised in a wider field, and that you work just as fruit-
fully as you could in your Congregation for the glory of
God and the salvation of souls. For this reason his Holiness releases you and dispenses you from the vow by which
you have bound yourself in accordance with the rules of
your Institute not to accept such a dignity. You must, therefore, consider it certain that such is the firm purpose of the
Holy Father. You will, I have no doubt, respond with religious obedience, meanwhile taking your own time for
the canonical examination.[7]

The Nuncio had also included a more personal letter stating:

"I am certain that you will bow your head under the burden which the Head of the Church imposes upon you. We all know that you did not desire the episcopate, and we are sincerely impressed by your refusal. But permit me to say further that resistance would be resistance to the will of God. You do not know what God may have in store, or the good that may result from your election for both your diocese and your Congregation. Every thing possible was done to promote your petition, yet the Pontiff persisted in his resolution, all of which indicates that the decision comes from the Holy Spirit. I await your answer so as to transmit it to the Holy Father."[8]

Alphonsus carefully read each letter for a second time and handed them back to Mazzini. "Gloria Patri!" Alphonsus almost whispered. "Since the Pope wishes me to be a bishop, then I wish to be a bishop."[9]

He fastened his will to the will of God with all the strength he possessed, but every one of his human faculties rebelled at the burden. The shock of realization that followed brought on a serious crisis and his colleagues once again feared for his life. Fever reduced him to delirium, and over and over again he begged his companions: "Do not forget me. After living together for thirty years, we are to be separated. Do not forget me." As the fever intensified, his mind fixed on the idea that God was driving him out of the Congregation because of his unworthiness. Nothing served to console him.

Two days later he managed to begin initial preparations in spite of his fever. Writing to his brother, Hercules, he revealed part of the spirit that was to characterize his approach to his new responsibilities.

Nocera
March 21, 1762

My dear Brother,

I have been so amazed by the command which I have received from the Pope to accept the episcopate out of obedience that I am stupefied at the thought of having to leave the Congregation where I have lived for thirty years. ...I thank you for offering to lend me the money necessary to pay expenses. If you had not offered to do so I would have written to the Pope, because I have no means of paying for necessary expenses.

...About the carriage, yes I shall have to get one, but I want to see whether the former bishop has left a usable one because I could get it very cheaply....This week or next I shall be in Naples and then we can talk.

You are rejoicing and I do nothing but lament. How was it that the episcopate was reserved for me in my old age? But may the divine will be always done, which wishes me to be a martyr in the last years of my life. I have lost sleep and appetite.

Your lordship's affectionate brother,
Alfonso

P.S. Today, Sunday, I am not very well. This morning an attack of fever came on and this evening, when I write, it has not yet left me.[10]

The fever became even more intense as each day passed and on the following Saturday, March 27, holy Viaticum was brought to the cell of Alphonsus. Rumor immediately traveled to Rome that the holy bishop-elect had died. Yet three days later, Alphonsus emerged from his cell and continued preparation for the trip to Naples!

When the day of his departure arrived, his confessor, Father Villani, had to resort to pressure to persuade him to leave behind his threadbare habit and old shoes, and to shave the ragged beard that had become one of his "trademarks." When others insisted that such an appearance was unbecoming the dignity of the office of bishop, he replied only that he did not see why a bishop should cease living a life of poverty and humility.

More than one letter to old friends in Naples revealed the hopes he still harbored for a reprieve from the pope. Writing to Mother Mary Graziano, he confided:

I have great hopes from my journey to Rome. People now call me "Most Illustrious," but let them wait. When the Pope sees me, old and infirm as I am, I shall have no need to plead, for he himself will say to me: "Go away, the mitre is not made for heads like yours."[11]

Before he left Naples for Rome he visited a jeweler to arrange for his episcopal ring and pectoral cross. After looking in dismay at several samples thrust at him by the eager Neopolitan shopkeeper, he left specific instructions for the jeweler to follow. His choice was simple: a ring of glass and a simple iron cross. Both would serve to remind him of his ambition to serve the poor always and to be a bishop of the poor.

On April 20 Alphonsus began a journey to Rome that would take five days. When he finally arrived in the Holy City, the weary old man went to the feet of the Apostle, Saint Peter, to beg his intercession and guidance in the days that stretched before him.

When word of his arrival reached official circles, Alphonsus found himself deluged with distinguished visitors and invitations to appear as guest of honor at special receptions and dinners. It had been over forty-five years since his father, Don Joseph, had arranged a similar whirl of activities, hoping to arrange a suitable marriage. The parallel could not have been entirely lost on Alphonsus.

He received the guests who came to offer congratulations, assuring each of them, as he did Abate Bruni: "I possess none of the qualifications necessary for the episcopate; but I bow my head under the orders of the Pope, for God wills us to obey Him." He declined almost all of the invitations he received. When the Vincentians repeatedly extended invitations to dinner, he replied simply: "Please give to the poor of Jesus Christ the dinner you wish to offer me so that Our Lord will reveal to me in Rome his holy will."[12] When he was unable to avoid acceptance of a formal invitation, he appeared dressed simply in the cassock of a Redemptorist rather than in his episcopal robes.

After only three days in Rome he wrote to Hercules:

It seems as though I have already been here a thousand years. I am so anxious to escape from public appearances, and especially from ceremonies because the gifts involved are bankrupting me. There is an unbelievable amount of ceremony, but it costs an unbelievable amount of money.[13]

Pope Clement XIII granted him audience early in May, and Alphonsus once again spoke of the three reasons he felt unable to fulfill the obligation that was being thrust upon him: 1) age; 2) poor health; 3) lack of capacity. Clement only answered: "Obedience works miracles; trust in God and God will help you."[14]

On June 14, 1762, Don Alphonsus de Liguori was consecrated bishop of the church of the Minerva by Cardinal Ferdinand Rossi, Archbishop Innocent Giorgoni, and Archbishop Dominic Giordani. Alphonsus later confessed to Father Villani that this was the saddest day of his life. "I had to struggle with myself," he admitted, "to accept a responsibility that frightened me."[15] But once the responsibility rested on his shoulder, he immediately began preparations to go to his people.

Before leaving for St. Agata, he received an account of the expenses involved in preparing the formal documents and conducting the ceremonies of his consecration. His response was blunt: "I did not ask for the episcopate. The only way I could possibly pay these charges is to use the revenues of my church, and I must use these to help the poor."[16] No further requests for payment were made.

On June 21 Alphonsus celebrated Mass in the church of St. Ignatius and then left Rome for Naples. For eight days he was again surrounded by nobility and members of the hierarchy eager to pay their respects to the new bishop. Some of them had slammed their doors in his face years before when he came to them begging for support for his Congregation, but they had, of course, forgotten such shadows as they showered official compliments on the celebrated Monsignor Liguori.

A priest from the town of Arienzo visiting in Naples presented himself to his new bishop reeking of perfume, sporting a curled and powdered wig, and shoes with shiny silver buckles. Alphonsus sadly shook his head. "My son," he said, "neither your shoes nor your hair-style become a priest."[17] Soon after, Alphonsus set out for Nocera on his way to St. Agata.

Late in the evening of July 3, he arrived at Pagani and was

soon surrounded by old friends whose greeting was far more sincere than that of the Neopolitan nobility. He blessed each of them with tears in his eyes.

A plan had been devised in his absence to permit him to continue as rector major without crippling the operations of the rapidly expanding Congregation. Father Villani had subsequently been appointed by the consultors to present to Pope Clement XIII a formal petition.

> Most Holy Father, it has pleased your Holiness to nominate to the See of St. Agata Don Alphonsus de Liguori, the founder and mainstay of our Congregation. It would, therefore, devolve on us to replace him by another perpetual Rector. But his rule has resulted in so many advantages spiritual and temporal for the Institute that we all unanimously desire to confirm him in the office of Rector Major; first, in order that our Congregation may continue to progress under his direction, and then to give our father a well-deserved testimony of our veneration and gratitude. In this case the government would be exercised by him through a Vicar General of his own choosing, with all the powers of the Rector Major in ordinary matters, but with the obligation of consulting and obeying him in grave matters, such as the dismissal of a subject, or the founding or abandoning of a house.[18]

On May 25, 1762, the Congregation of Bishops granted the petition, and Alphonsus, overjoyed at the news that he would be permitted to continue his relationship with his beloved Institute, named Father Villani as vicar general of the Congregation.

After five short days Alphonsus insisted on beginning the journey to St. Agata. In spite of his longing to linger awhile among friends and brothers, he said goodbye to all of them on June 8, 1762. His parting words touched those who heard them deeply. "Goodbye beloved brothers," he said. "Do not forget your poor exile, for to live away from you is to live in exile....I am saying goodbye to you but I shall come back to die at St. Michael's."[19]

When the weary bishop at last reached his diocese, he went at once to his cathedral and knelt in prayer before his beloved Lord in the Blessed Sacrament. The people of St. Agata, who had eagerly awaited the arrival of the famous missionary who was to be their bishop, had crowded the cathedral to hear him speak to them for the first time. Turning slowly toward them, he began to speak sincerely, assuring them that he had not come to St. Agata looking for a comfortable life; he had come instead to draw all of them to the feet of Christ by his word and work and example. He had come to serve and not to rule, and he begged the priests and religious present to share his burden. Finally, he announced that he would personally conduct a general mission in the diocese that would begin within a week of his arrival.

Before he could finish, Alphonsus found himself unable to continue because of a severe attack of coughing brought on by his chronic respiratory difficulties, which was undoubtedly hastened by the fatigue and anxiety connected with his travels. Several minutes later the attack subsided a little and he managed to conclude the short service with formal Benediction.

Shortly after leaving the cathedral, Alphonsus entered his new episcopal mansion and discovered a mound of gifts presented to him as tokens of welcome by the many religious communities and noblemen of the area. He thanked each of them warmly but promptly returned each of the gifts, firmly announcing his policy of never accepting such gifts.

When he appeared at the dinner table, he could not believe his eyes. His new and zealous secretary had organized a formal banquet in his honor, and the table was crowded with foods of all kinds. Before sitting down, he summoned the secretary, Felix Verzella, and heatedly asked: "Do you think I came here to give banquets when the poor go hungry?"[20] As long as he remained at St. Agata, his table consisted of vegetable soup and a little boiled beef, to which one other dish was added for visitors.

This custom was the subject of a great deal of ridicule within the household and partially accounted for the reluctance of some to accept invitations to share in the bishop's table.

The following day Alphonsus inspected every room of the house, directing the immediate removal of furniture that seemed to contradict a spirit of poverty and humility. When he decided which of the rooms was the least comfortable, he made it his own. Servants, indignant at the unusual conduct of their new employer, wasted no time describing his attitude in the marketplace, but rather than ridicule, the news produced the growing conviction that the new bishop was truly "a bishop of the poor."

Two years after assuming responsibility for his new diocese, Alphonsus drafted his first report to the Sacred Congregation in Rome. His summary of the work he managed to do in such a short time, and his simple description of the diocese, seem much more fitting here than any possible secondhand account:

> St. Agata, situated on a table-land surrounded by mountains, down whose side rush wild torrents, is said to have derived its name from the Goths, who in early times sought refuge here and is by no means an insignificant city. It belongs to the kingdom of Naples and is subject to the feudal tenure of the Duke of Maddaloni. It is in the province known as "Beyond the Mountains" and occupies a central position in the diocese.
>
> ...The cathedral is under the title of the Assumption of the Blessed Virgin. It was consecrated in 1763 and is subject to the metropolitan of Benevento.
>
> Besides the episcopal city, the diocese comprises many cities and towns: Arienzo, situated in Campania; Felix, with its suburbs, the second city of the diocese; Arpaia and its dependency Forchia, so-called from the passage of the Caudine Forks; Airola, raised to the rank of a city a few years ago; and Pastorano. A fifth city is Frasso, another Valle, and lastly Durrazano, with its dependencies.
>
> ...Among the charitable institutions of the city of St. Agata there are only two, under the title of Saint Anne, for the relief of the poor.
>
> The seminary, which adjoins the episcopal residence, is being built almost from the foundations in more spacious proportions. The amount spent so far on its construction is about 5,000 gold ducats Neopolitan currency. In the course of a few years, I think, this great work will be finished. The seminarians, meanwhile, are housed in

some buildings belonging to my residence which have been converted into a temporary seminary. The seventy seminarians were received, after examination, from all parts of the city and diocese. They are under the guidance of very competent masters in various fields, who instruct them thoroughly, especially in scholastic theology. I pay unexpected visits to the seminary from time to time to make sure that it is conducted properly and to gauge progress in studies.

...There is in the city a convent of Our Lady of Constantinople which has been completed during my term of office. It has all the necessary living and workrooms and a church nearby. Up to the present, however, no sisters have been received. One thing still remains, and it is indeed a matter of no small consequence, namely, that the Sacred Congregation of Bishops and Regulars accede to my request and permit me to unite for the upkeep of this foundation the revenues of some holy places in the city, as the present income of the convent is, of course, quite unequal to the demands of the institution. It remains also for the Congregation to allow the reception of nuns in this convent; and, finally, to grant a petition already submitted by them to the municipal authorities, asking permission to change this conservatory into a convent with enclosure under a Rule already approved by the Sacred Congregation. (The request was made in the name of the nuns of the Most Holy Redeemer and was granted. On June 29, 1766, four nuns from Scala took possession of the convent.)

I should not forget to mention that I am building, in the district of Arienzo for the greater convenience of the people, a new parish church dedicated to Saint Nicholas. It is on a more suitable site and will be very large and beautiful. This work goes on in spite of continual contentions between the municipal authorities and the citizens, which I have done everything I could to quell. In the course of two years, with the help of God, this

church will probably be completed so that the old building, which is completely ruined and also too small, may
be abandoned.

I have also given a great deal of attention to the repair
of the other churches in the diocese: the church of St. Agnes
and the church of St. Peter in Talanico, both of which
have been provided with new walls and new flooring.

…The number of persons in Sant Agata and its suburbs is about 5,200; in Arienzo and its dependencies, more
than 10,000; in Arpaia and Furchia, 1,600; in Airola and
its dependencies, 6,200; in Frasso, 2,600; in Valle, 1,000;
in Bagnoli, 250; in Dugenta, over 300; and in Cancello,
about 200.

The secular clergy of the city and suburbs number
about 80 priests: Arienzo has 20; Airola, about 80; Valle,
about 30. In the baronies with the exception of Bagnoli,
which has one priest recently ordained, there are no priests
at present and no prospect of receiving any increase from
these quarters. The people there live the life of farmers.

…As a body, the clergy, with a few exceptions, I have
found to be well disposed. Their manners, however, are
not altogether what they ought to be although now, by
means of the spiritual exercises which they are required
to attend every year, there is, thanks be to God, marked
improvement among them. For the most part, they are
very deficient in the necessary knowledge of theology, particularly Moral Theology. There are, however, exceptions
to this rule; some indeed are very learned men. To remedy
this situation as best I could, I have established academies
of Moral Theology for the instruction of those who lack
the necessary knowledge, and I have placed at their head
learned priests of my own selection.

By the grace of God, my entire flock has been provided for during my term of office with missions given at
frequent intervals in the city and throughout the diocese
by the fathers of my own Congregation of the Most Holy
Redeemer, by the most zealous missionaries of Father
Pavone of Naples, and by the Pious Workers. The people

are well instructed in the faith and conscientious in their attendance at Mass.

I animate the zeal of my parish priests in every way. As far as I can perceive they are doing their duty well, preaching the Gospel to the people every Sunday and holy day, teaching the children, boys and girls, administering the sacraments to the sick, and fulfilling all the other obligations of their office to the best of their ability.

During Lent the word of God is preached daily in the cathedral....For the discharge of this duty only those are chosen who preach the Word of God in a simple and popular style, ignoring any temptation to engage in rhetoric and who aim only to preach Jesus Christ crucified.

...Since my coming the practice of mental prayer and the devotion to the Blessed Virgin Mary, particularly on Saturdays, have been everywhere encouraged. Every Saturday also, in order to increase the devotion of the faithful towards the Mother of God, a sermon is preached in her honor by some pious and learned priest whom I myself select.

Every year in company with the Vicar-General, I conduct the Canonical Visitation of one-half of the diocese and, in accordance with the desire of the Council of Trent, I repeat the same before the completion of two years, to aid me in the discharge of my duty. I am careful to summon to my assistance the members of my own Congregation, the Missionary Priests of the Most Holy Redeemer. These Fathers have done much to advance the spiritual welfare of the people by frequent missions in the city, and even more throughout the diocese....

I have also been careful to frequently administer the sacrament of Confirmation. And when not prevented by my health, which has been very poor for some time, I officiate at the times prescribed and perform the other functions of my episcopal office. I have not been absent from my diocese at all, and am quite content to take up my residence in the future within its boundaries.

At times I have been present in choir at the cathedral

to give good example to the canons and to encourage their fervor in the devout recitation of the Divine Office.

Daily I offer up the Holy Sacrifice of the Mass for the flock confided to my care and publicly and privately assist with money and food the poor, especially those who are sick and those whose virtue is in peril, and fallen women, that they might be kept from sin.

...What I have said is about all I think necessary to lay before the Sacred Congregation. If in my report there is anything that calls for censure, I am prepared most humbly to receive their corrections, and bow my head in respectful submission.

Your most humble, devoted and obedient servant,

Alfonso Maria
Bishop of Sant' Agata of the Goths[21]

How can we sift the records of the past and touch the heart of a man? Official accounting of the years Alphonsus labored among the people of St. Agata somehow produces a rather blurred image of him. One aspect that emerges is that of a competent administrator who structured his time well and built a few buildings that were not there before. But is this all that remains?

The diocese of St. Agata was not very large by modern standards. The people were generally poor and wedded to the land that enslaved them. The currents that were soon to explode into the age of revolution were all there: general levels of poverty, mistrust of the motives of the clergy, and the intensely human desire to reap more than was sown. Rationalists mockingly spoke of the army of priests whose only solution for the problem of hunger was a novena for bread.

What did Alphonsus do about the poor? His approach was always personal and compassionate; always more concerned with the needs of the one who approached him than with details of background or proofs of worth. He visited the homes of the poor himself, noting the needs of those who were too ashamed to ask openly for help.

No period in the career of Alphonsus placed such demands on his love of the poor than the time that the history of southern

Italy refers to as the "great famine."[22] It was the winter of 1763 when the first signs of coming disaster began to appear. Wheat withered and died on the stalk, leaving only parched signs of what should have been in fields throughout the mountains. Vegetables that might have provided an alternate diet for the mountain people never lasted until harvest...and hunger drove many toward the cities in hopes of finding the bread there they could not find at home. Their hopes were soon vanquished and roads to major cities were clogged with those who came to beg bread from those who had none.

By midsummer the situation was desperate and some chronicles of the period speak of outbreaks of cannibalism and related atrocities. Those who hoarded food were in peril as they attempted to defend what they had gathered from those who were willing to sacrifice anything to preserve their own existence. Before the scourge had ended, hundreds of thousands of persons had perished.

St. Agata was far from the sea, far from the hope that a passing ship would stop to unload at least a temporary supply of grain or beans. The mountains shut out hope for many, and the many turned to the bishop of the flock.

"Give to everyone," he instructed, "they are only asking for what belongs to them." But before long Alphonsus too was without supplies. Frantically he negotiated for more grain and dried vegetables, using any influence he might have to obtain the needed provisions. Small quantities of grain came from Naples, thanks to the intercession of Alphonsus' brother, Hercules. Supplies could be had in other places if one was willing to pay a high enough price, and Alphonsus paid the price. When his revenues were gone, he borrowed money from friends. When the borrowed funds were gone, he tried to engineer a loan from business interests that would enable him to purchase enough supplies to permit him to feed all the hungry who came to his door until the new crop could be harvested. No one would lend it to him. Alphonsus was, to put it quite simply, a bad risk!

His ragged appearance did nothing to inspire the confidence of the businessmen to whom he applied for aid. And, finally, his refusal in the past to court the favor of the wealthy did nothing to gain him their cooperation in this crisis. He had no personal assets; he was old and admitted he was at the door of death itself.

Alphonsus did not abandon hope but the chance of doing anything at all seemed slender. If no one would lend him money, he would do what he had to do. And so he began to sell what little he had, but it brought next to nothing. There was only one thing left that would bring anything at all, and his previous attempts to dispose of it had met with no success at all. The carriage that he had purchased secondhand from the bishop who preceded him (and which still bore the coat of arms of the former bishop because Alphonsus felt it would be too costly to have a new one made) was still in the coach house. Everyone on his staff had insisted that he must retain the carriage because of his weak health, and besides, a bishop could not very well walk to his appointments! "Saint Peter was Pope," he answered, "yet he never rode in a carriage. It seems to me that I am not greater than Saint Peter."[23]

When he enlisted the help of Hercules in trying to sell the carriage in Naples, his brother, too, agreed with those who discouraged him from the sale. But Alphonsus had made up his mind. Writing to Hercules (November 28, 1763), he insisted:

> ...I am old and have one foot in the grave, I am burdened with debts; I should take on many expenses necessary for the glory of God, and I am grieved to death that I cannot because I must first pay the debts that I owe you and the seminary. I beg of you, therefore, not to trouble me any more about this or I will no longer answer your letters....
>
> If you do not wish to do me the favor to sell the mules and carriage at a suitable time, as I cannot throw them into the street, I will ask the help of someone else and I will get rid of them at any price.
>
> Your letter causes me pain. I cannot stand to see the mules standing for a whole year in the stable while the coachman is in the tavern and the poor are crying for mercy and I have nothing to give to them....[24]

In January of the new year, the mules and carriage were sent to Naples to be sold to the highest bidder. His brother, Cajetan, having learned from Hercules of the intentions of his brother, purchased the carriage himself. But the price could do little to feed the numbers who were without food. The growing unrest was creating a situation that bordered on anarchy. Aware of the political unrest, Alphonsus appealed to the highest civil authority, the Duke of Maddaloni, to help stem the tide of hunger (January 26, 1774).

> Your excellency should know that we are in great fear here because the lack of bread has reached such a point that we are every day in danger of seeing people rising in revolt, for the people, even with money in their hands, do not find any grain or bread to buy....I do all that I can to help these poor people. I have already sold my carriage and the mules which I owned and I also plan on going into debt, but I know that I cannot succeed in doing what I hope to do and I constantly tremble, waiting for a revolution, since several times the people have erupted into violence....Again, I beg your Excellency to bring your grain here to support your distressed subjects who, without this aid, would be reduced to despair....[25]

The Duke listened to Alphonsus, but many supplies that came from this source somehow fell into the hands of black marketeers.

Alphonsus fasted because there were those who had no bread. "When people are dying of hunger," he said more than once, "everyone should fast." The daily menu on his own table never exceeded a small quantity of soup and a little boiled beef during this period. He met with the superiors of all the religious houses in the diocese to try to encourage them to fast within their own communities so that they might contribute more to the poor. His challenge was taken up by many religious.

Everywhere Alphonsus looked he thought he found something to sell so that he could buy bread for his beloved poor, but others followed after him to insist that he was impractical and that what he wanted to sell had little or no value. When he picked up his pastoral staff, he would think of selling it. A small gem on the clasp of the cope he used for ceremonial occasions caught his eye, and he asked that it be sold. A silver basin and pitcher used in the cathedral during Mass seemed a likely item to go on the block, but the cathedral canons who held jurisdiction over the property would not permit him to dispose of it.

Alphonsus wept and he wept bitterly. "My God," he pleaded, "why can't I be like Saint Thomas Villanova? He found granaries full of corn when he needed them."[26] He doubled his personal fast and assumed new penitential obligations in the hopes of some-how turning the tide of hopelessness that swept the countryside until spring came at last, and the sight of new crops brought new hope. The crisis had passed at last.

"The bishop," he had so often said during those trying months, "must think of the poor who have no one to dry their tears. They are special members of Jesus Christ."[27] Sometimes this conviction led to responses that were more impulsive than practical. On sev-eral occasions he found himself physically unable to eat because he was so aware of the poverty of those who came to his door. "How do you expect me to go on eating while they have no bread?" he would ask. And then he would insist that his own lunch be brought to them.

Many of his friends and almost all of those who worked with him insisted that he was constantly being used by people who did not really deserve his charity. His response was characteristic: "You are probably right," he would admit, "but it is better to be tricked into giving too much than to risk one's soul by not giving enough."[28] They listened to him but they did not hear. The more that others insisted that he should only help the honest poor, the more he insisted: "I must help all the poor, but especially those whom help might save from sin."

The following year, as Alphonsus approached his seventieth birthday, he resolved to resign from his position as bishop. His health, which had been wretched when he assumed the grave re-sponsibility of heading the diocese, had grown steadily worse. Each of the three years he had labored in the mountains had pro-duced a major illness that had brought him close to death. Every chronic condition that assailed him in the past returned now to plague him, and sometimes several sufferings combined to intensify his pain. Yet he was not yet sure that God willed his resignation. As always when in doubt about a serious decision, he consulted those whose opinion he valued most highly. After consulting Monsignor Borgia in Naples, who assured him that under the circumstances it would seem that God willed his retirement, he wrote to Father Villani (January 14, 1765) outlining the nature of his own doubts.

> ...My strong inclination urges me to resign because I see myself oppressed by so many thoughts of scruples, scandals, and the many requests I have to refuse. But then I tremble more because I am afraid that in resigning I am seeking my own convenience and not the glory of God.[29]

On February 1, 1765, Alphonsus sent Villani a lengthy letter that thoroughly explained every aspect of the situation and again revealed his own hesitation to seek release.

> Live Jesus, Mary, Joseph
> (read this privately)
> ...My Dear Don Andrew, I wish to have a peaceful conscience.
> It is true that the problems I have encountered here, and the many qualms of conscience that plague me, lead me to hope for the freedom to enjoy a little peace and quiet. But I do not want my cell to later become a hell on earth because I have freed myself from my burden in opposition to God's will.
> I am certain that God willed me to become a bishop three years ago. Now, before I free myself, I must be morally certain that He wishes me to be a bishop no longer....
> It is necessary to bear in mind that, according to Saint Thomas, a bishop is bound by vow not to leave his church and the Pope says he cannot leave it without just cause. Among the causes he expressly says are insufficient are pressure of fatigue and love of solitude. The reasons most appropriate for me to state, then, would be old age and

bad health; but it is necessary to note that the Pope also says that infirmity and old age excuse only when they make a subject unfit to exercise his office....

...It is true that I am old, since next September I shall reach seventy. I also have bad health but in spite of this I do not fail to do my duty. ...It is true that in the winter I cannot go out but during the summer I never fail to make the rounds of the diocese for four or five months. During the winter, even though I do not go out, I manage to carry on official business and write letters. I cannot often hold a pen, but I make use of my confidential secretary, Brother Francis Romito, whom I trust.

...I pray to Jesus Christ continually to make His will known to me. When I weigh all the evidence I have put down above, it does not seem to me that I can resign without scruples that will later rise to haunt me.

...I want to add that the dampness of the climate here at St. Agata during the winter is very bad for me. But I have thought of spending next winter at Arienzo, which is warmer and drier.

This state of anxiety over whether I am doing God's will by resigning pains me more than anything else at this point.

Live Jesus and Mary. I have been ill for many days with asthma but I am now better.

Brother Alfonso Maria
of the Most Holy Redeemer,
Bishop of St. Agata[30]

After weighing the evidence presented to him, Villani decided that Alphonsus could, in good conscience, ask to be relieved of his office and so he drew up a formal petition to Pope Clement XIII. Months passed and no answer arrived from Rome to settle the matter. Finally, on June 18, 1765, Cardinal Megroni, whom Pope Clement had appointed to communicate his decision, addressed the following reply to the aging bishop:

...His Holiness thanks God for all the good you have,

by the grace of God, accomplished up to this point; and it would be a cause of great pain to him to deprive your people of the good you will yet do by your authority and good example, even though your illness might become worse and your strength continue to diminish (God forbid!). His Holiness has, therefore, asked me to tell you to put aside all scruples and to work as you have always done, with perfect peace of mind, for the salvation of souls entrusted to your care, and for the glory of God who will surely give you all the help you need.[31]

The reaction of Alphonsus was that of a man conditioned to accept the will of God as soon as it was revealed to him: "Well," he sighed, "let us continue to be a bishop since God wills it so." His doctor, obviously displeased at the news, demanded that he at least change residence during the winter months in the hope of averting another medical crisis. The weary bishop relented at last and agreed to live at Arienzo, another of the major centers of the diocese. As soon as the decision was made public, difficulties multiplied. Writing to Father Villani (June 26, 1765), he outlined his own objections.

At St. Agata they are much displeased that I must go to live at Arienzo next winter; and I myself am displeased because my cathedral is there, my chancery is there, and above all my seminary is there.[32]

In mid-October, Alphonsus departed for Arienzo in spite of the misgivings that weighed heavily on his heart. The climate was certainly not as damp and cold as that at St. Agata in the mountains. But, in spite of the change, violent attacks of asthma kept him confined to bed for weeks at a time. In early spring (April 27, 1766) Alphonsus wrote:

As soon as the weather permits me to escape, I should go back to St. Agata. It seems a thousand years since I left.[33]

Year after year the holy bishop struggled to fulfill the ideal he had set for himself as pastor, yet things seemed to always slip beyond his grasp. By June of 1768 he was once again stricken with severe illness. Intense pain traveled up and down his right side and finally settled in his right hip. His sense of frustration must have been acute, but he managed to write to Sister Brianna Carafa (June 25, 1768):

> I must have been in bed for fifteen days and have been unable to say Mass. Pray to Jesus Christ for me so that I might unite myself completely to His Holy will. Never forget to pray for the Church.[34]

Writing to Father Villani four days later, he confessed:

> After many treatments, I remain in about the same condition except, perhaps, that I am in greater pain than ever. The doctors do not seem to know what to do next and so I have decided to leave things to God and to embrace as much pain as God wishes me to endure. In a few days I shall travel to St. Agata for my visitation.[35]

Early in June he wrote once again to Brianna.

> ...After the night comes the day. But the only day we should desire in this life is that day when we shall see and love God face to face. Pray to Jesus Christ for me; I lie in this bed like a piece of wood. Let us pray always: My dear Jesus, I long to suffer for you.[36]

By the end of August his condition was so serious that he made out his will: two hours after his death, all his possessions were to be distributed to the poor. Officials of the diocese even went so far as to plan the route of his funeral procession. But once again death failed to claim Alphonsus. Father Mazzini, who was close to Alphonsus during these days of intense suffering, informed the convent at Scala of his condition, closing with a note of hope:

Our Father is burning with fever and must remain in a chair since he cannot go to bed. He does not celebrate Mass; he cannot even say the Rosary. Everything seems to suggest that Our Lord plans to call him to Himself, yet we continue to pray and pray that he will stay with us a little longer for the glory of God and the good of our beloved Congregation. As for me, I am now an unprofitable servant because of my infirmity. I pray that Our Lord might shorten my life if I could somehow prolong that of our beloved Father.

P.S. Good news this morning. He is able to eat a little and to sleep for a few minutes. This is an improvement![37]

Alphonsus lived for nineteen more years, but they would be years of continual martyrdom. The disease traveled from his hip to his spine and spread throughout his body. Finally, it affected the vertebrae in his neck, bending it so much that his chin rested permanently on his chest. The pressure caused by his chin produced a deep wound that easily became infected. Dr. Mauro, who treated him during this period commented:

Witnessing his peace we felt pain had no power over him. Even if his only pain were the wound in his chest that was infected to the bone, it would have been enough to drive another person mad. Never once did I hear him complain.[38]

By October his condition improved slightly but he confided to Father Villani (October 8, 1765):

The nights are all like days. Nature rebels but I think I am united to the will of God. Remember me when you celebrate your Mass so that God will give me perfect resignation.[39]

Throughout the reign of Pope Clement XIII, Alphonsus attempted to fulfill every demand made on him as bishop, in spite of the continual pain that tormented him. When Clement XIV

assumed the papacy in 1769, Alphonsus, with the blessing of his
director, Father Villani, once again laid his tentative request for
relief from this pastoral duty at his doorstep. His response tested
the old man once more. The pope was aware of the condition of
Bishop Liguori but decided:

> I am satisfied that he rule his diocese from his bed....His
> prayer will do more than all the activity in the world.[40]

Alphonsus was crushed. Many other bishops and friends advised him to submit a formal resignation which would in all prob-
ability receive a different response. But he replied after prayer:
"The voice of the Pope is the voice of God for me. I will die happy
if I die crushed by the will of God."

Two years later Pope Clement XIV was dead. While awaiting
word of the identity of the pope's successor, Alphonsus bared his
heart to his friend and director, Father Villani (November 9, 1774).

> The thought of resigning has returned to me. Read my
> letter carefully and pray to Jesus Christ about it. I do not
> want to act out of self-will but to do what God really
> wants.
>
> On one hand, the torture that I suffer in ruling a dio-
> cese is too great. Sick and crippled and unable to get
> around, I am tormented by scruples about everything so
> that I long to go and die in the Congregation.
>
> On the other hand, my Vicar General is quite respon-
> sible about filling in for me. And, although I am a cripple,
> my mind is still clear, and I manage to do a great deal by
> correspondence....
>
> I think I can help the interests of the Congregation
> more by remaining by my charge than by leaving it. This
> is my sorrow. On the one hand I want to go and rest, and
> on the other, if I rest, it seems to me that I could not do
> half of what I do as bishop. For now I place the problem
> before God and ask your Reverence to pray about it. When
> you come back we will discuss the matter because I want
> only what God wants.[41]

Villani counseled him that he was not only free to submit his resignation in good conscience, but that he was probably bound to do so for the good of the Congregation. But Alphonsus was racked with anxiety.

> This thought that I am abandoning my Church in order to leave my cross behind makes me very anxious. Encourage me by showing me that I am doing the will of God.[42]

In April 1775, he submitted his formal resignation to Pope Pius VI saying, in part:

> I am in extreme old age, for in the month of September I enter my eightieth year. Besides old age, I have many illnesses that warn me that death is near...during my episcopate I have received Viaticum four times and Extreme Unction twice.
>
> Besides, other difficulties prevent me from fulfilling my obligations as bishop. My hearing is seriously failing so that many people suffer who want to speak to me privately. I am so paralyzed that I can barely write a line. I sign my name only with difficulty and so badly that it is almost impossible to read. I have become so crippled that I am no longer able to walk a step. I spend my life in bed or alone in a chair. I can no longer ordain priests or preach.
>
> For these reasons I think myself obliged, seeing myself near death, to beg your Holiness to accept my resignation as Bishop....[43]

The resignation was accepted. Alphonsus de Liguori was at long last once again a simple Redemptorist.

CHAPTER 7

The Journey's End

Alphonsus breathed a slow sigh of relief as he was helped into his chair by a lay brother. After so many years of exile, he was once again in his own cell at Pagani, and he rejoiced when he realized that he was home at last. Some people had laughed a little to themselves as they watched him leave St. Agata followed by all his earthly possessions: a wooden cross, a copper lamp, and a candlestick. But the vast majority of those who lined both sides of the road as far as the eye could see would miss their bishop. Many were not ashamed to weep.

The old man thought of them now—those who wept and those who were glad to be rid of him—and he scooped them up into a single prayer.

Alphonsus was a complete cripple for the remaining twelve years of his life, but his heart still burned to draw others closer to Jesus. At least once a week he spoke to the Congregation, exhorting them bluntly again and again: "What are we doing here if we are not trying to become saints?" His love for the poor was as ardent as ever; personally he listened to their needs and visited them whenever possible to console them in their suffering. But few, if any, were able to console Alphonsus in the trials he was about to undergo.

When Alphonsus returned to resume his role as permanent rector major, the Congregation was on the brink of ruin. Forces at Naples led by the Marquis Tannuci planned to dissolve the Institute, not out of vengeance, but out of misguided zeal for the good of the kingdom of Naples.

On the other hand, the reputation of the tiny band of missionaries was improving. People spoke glowingly of the small group of men who had planned to work only among the very poorest of people in outlying districts, but who had the ear of even the nobility. Tannuci remembered that the Jesuits, too, had had humble beginnings and that their power had become so great that they had recently been suppressed forcibly in many countries in Europe. He had, in fact, been instrumental in their suppression throughout the kingdom.

On February 13, 1777, a report was submitted to the king by the royal procurator recommending complete dissolution of the Institute.[1] The report read in part:

After a careful study of the Rule of the Most Holy Redeemer, I have found it to be quite similar to the rule of the Jesuits....In the Superior General I recognize the despot who held complete authority over the Society. The essence of the Jesuit system was that the General was absolute Master...that was the secret of Jesuit government and the factor that made the Society such a threat. It is noteworthy that the Rule states that members are to concentrate on preaching the Gospel to poor abandoned souls but then goes on to speak of spiritual exercises for priests and laity and of preaching in missionary churches. The Jesuits also began humbly but wound up monopolizing everything—preaching, spiritual exercises, schools, seminaries, from which they were able to recruit followers without number. This is what will be done by the so-called followers of the Most Holy Redeemer.

...Liguorian theology relies completely on Jesuit authors. It adopts their fundamental principles with fatal consequences...these doctrines are so dangerous that they impel me to beg your Majesty to take the most secure steps to crush them utterly.

If the ambition of certain priests who aspire to the title of founders (an ambition which has always led men to the greatest excesses), if such ambition tends to corrupt morals, your Majesty must use every means in his power to stamp out the evil.

The worst things have had fair beginnings. No new sect has ever sprung up without disguising itself under the appearance of good, but time has always revealed that fanaticism, ambition and singularity have been the primary motives of their founders.

The report concluded with the following recommendations to the king of Naples:

His Majesty should appoint some sound theologians to examine the Moral Theology of Alphonsus de Liguori, and after noting the countless errors the work contains that could easily corrupt Christian morality, forbid all the members of his community to read it.

Secondly, until this examination is finished, the missionaries should not be permitted to hear confessions or preach.

Thirdly, they should be denied all rights that properly constitute a Congregation—superiors, house of studies, novitiate, privileges and property.

Finally, the property now possessed by them, except what might be claimed by individuals, should be sold and the proceeds invested so that the interest might be paid to ordained members during their lives. The other members, especially the novices, should be sent home.

The heart of Alphonsus was breaking. His life's dream was threatened beyond belief, and his reputation seemed to lie in ruins. But the aim of the procurator failed to hit its mark. The very person who would have implemented willingly the findings of the report, Marquis Tannuci, became the victim of an intrigue against his own power and fell unexpectedly from royal favor.[2]

In preparing a brief of appeal to the verdict of the Procurator Leone, Alphonsus still revealed the mind of a trained lawyer. He answered the charges made both against the Congregation and against his own motives as founder, point by point, being careful not to antagonize those who mistrusted him.

The most crucial area of the problem dealt with supposed violations of a royal decree issued in 1752 which forbade the foundation of any new religious orders in the kingdom. Alphonsus had, according to Procurator Leone, arbitrarily violated the decree in order to serve his own selfish ambition.

The reasoning of Alphonsus was simple. The rule in question had been approved by Pope Benedict XIV in 1749, three full years before the decree had been issued. Many of the articles, consequently, might *seem* to violate the decree while in fact these articles were not observed after the decree had been issued. (The articles in question dealt mainly with the acquisition of property.)

Leone had also insisted that the public profession of vows required by the rule constituted a religious order and was therefore a direct violation of the decree. Alphonsus, in turn, distinguished between simple and solemn vows, pointing out that the members of his Congregation did not profess solemn vows and, in fact, prohibited the formation of *any* Institute. So on this point, the security of the Congregation began to falter.

Rather than pursue an obviously weak point in his argument, Alphonsus, always the lawyer, changed the area of battle to another ground.

Bishops of the dioceses in which the houses of the Congregation were established wrote official letters to the king insisting that the missionaries were necessary to the spiritual well-being of their people. Influential friends of the fathers exerted pressure on their behalf whenever possible at court, yet many insisted that only Alphonsus' presence in Naples could turn the tide for victory. On September 2, 1777, Alphonsus replied once and for all to their plans.

Anyone who saw me in my present miserable state would not have the nerve to ask me to come to Naples to speak to the President, the Cardinal, Marquis Sambuca and Paoletti. My arrival would only help to collect a crowd of little lazzaroni around me to see if what was in the carriage was dead or alive. It is no use thinking about it, because I don't believe my trip would help the cause. If I spoke to the President he would contradict my very first word. Sambuca would simply stare at my bent neck and crippled body, and he would not understand what I would say because I can no longer manage to articulate properly. These are all beautiful dreams, but still dreams. I am ready to give my life to the Congregation but not by doing things which I think are useless. Let us put ourselves in the hands of God, who knows how to defend his own cause better than we do.[3]

For the time being, God did provide an answer to the problems of the Congregation in the form of an indefinite postponement of the case. But the fathers could not deceive themselves into thinking that their troubles were at an end. The cloud of possible destruction always hung over their heads. The next storm, Alphonsus knew well, could destroy the very foundations of the work.

If the Institute was to continue with any hope of stability, a base must be established outside the kingdom of Naples. The house at Beneventum was already outside its boundaries, but its isolated character offered no hope for the future. Alphonsus looked instead to the Papal States where the protection of the Holy See would prevent the eventual dissolution of the Congregation.

In spite of the difficulties involved in the transaction, and also his ever-failing health, Alphonsus began the necessary negotiations. The risks were great since the same royal decree that could lead to the legal dissolution of the Institute had also expressly limited the houses of the Congregation to four. The house at Beneventum had already been challenged by Procurator Leone as a deliberate violation of the law. The creation of another monastery could only strengthen the case for the opposition.

Yet, writing to Father de Paula at the foundation boldly undertaken at Scifelli in the Papal States on May 30, 1776, Alphonsus underlined his determination to insure the future of the Congregation at any cost.

...Let us speak clearly: if the Congregation does not establish itself outside the Kingdom of Naples it will never be a Congregation. Your Reverence has been given an extraordinary vocation by God to help his Congregation.

I am at the end of my life and but little time remains to
me. It is you who have to think of building it up.[4]

Father Francis de Paula, in whom Alphonsus placed so much
hope for the future of the Congregation, shared his hopes for more
houses in the Papal States. But the state of poverty and insecurity
in which the fathers of this foundation had to labor began to take
their toll on the young and zealous priest. Writing later to the
young superior at Scifelli, Alphonsus pleaded:

> I beg your Reverence as long as you hold the office of
> Superior there to be humble and courteous to all, espe-
> cially on the missions, and to show complete charity to
> our brethren. They find themselves in great physical pov-
> erty and far from Naples and their families, so you must
> be very, very charitable to them. I repeat this because your
> Reverence, while full of good intentions and good con-
> duct, has not good health. You are easily depressed and
> this makes you a burden to your colleagues. This was the
> only defect that was noticed in you when you were rector
> at St. Angelo.[5]

Unable to travel to the newly established houses himself,
Alphonsus sent as his visitor in the autumn of 1776 Father Peter
Paul Blasucci, a trusted friend and companion. When Father
Blasucci informed him of his safe arrival, Alphonsus replied (Oc-
tober 24, 1776):

> I imagine that I see our Congregation as a little ship in
> the midst of the sea, beaten on by many winds, and I am
> waiting for God to make known whether He wishes to
> bring it safely into the harbor. But if He wants us to see it
> sink I say now and always, "Blessed be His will forever…"
> I remain here continually praying for your Reverence that
> God will give you in those regions patience and light to
> carry His work to a good end if He wills it so. THE BE-
> GINNINGS THERE ARE WEAK BUT GOD CAN
> MAKE GREAT WORKS RISE FROM WEAK BEGIN-

NINGS; and I have confidence in Mary our Mother for those houses which are now so unstable.[6]

The future of the Congregation, then, lay in the hands of two men: de Paula, whom many thought too impulsive and too liberal, and Blasucci, whom many thought a little too prudent and too conservative. Loyalties within the Congregation, and especially within the newly established houses in the Papal States, began to align themselves unconsciously around these two figures. Early in 1777 Blasucci visited the houses at Scifelli and Frosinone. Writing to Alphonsus about Scifelli he observes:

> The members complain that up until now the observance of the Rule has left much to be desired. I have established regularity and the new superior will maintain it as he will preach by example.[7]

In regard to the financial situation of the monastery, he concluded:

> There has been a great deal of rashness, little prudence, and no circumspection. The badly equipped ship will be wrecked at the first storm. I write in riddles but you will understand me. We must place obstacles on this point.[8]

Eight houses of the Congregation now served the Church, four in the kingdom of Naples and four in the Papal States. In the midst of threats of suppression in Naples, Alphonsus pleaded with Blasucci to return to assist him. In his place as provincial of the houses of the Papal States, Alphonsus appointed de Paula.

Overwhelmed with the poverty and insecurity of the new foundations, de Paula wrote to Alphonsus asking for a large sum of money to aid him in reducing the debts under which they labored. Alphonsus answered candidly:

> At present I am living on love but I hope to get some money soon....In the meantime I beg you to remain completely at peace. When the foundations are beginning, you

must necessarily suffer poverty, confusion and opposition. But let us be completely resigned to the will of God.[9]

Although his communications with the houses to the north were severely hampered, Alphonsus never ceased thinking of them as his dream for the future of the Congregation. In a letter to all the fathers and brothers at Frosinone and Scifelli, he wrote (October, 1778):

> The houses of the Papal States should become the model of the true spirit of the Congregation to all other houses present or future. I do not wish you riches but only enough to live on, together with a love of the Rule which God has given you to make you saints, and to help you to bring others to sanctity.[10]

Months dragged on for the crippled old man, and still burdens heaped themselves on his head. Father de Paula began to consult Alphonsus less and less about the affairs of the Congregation to the north. Finally, on February 19, 1779, the rector major poured out his frustrations in a letter to de Paula.

> ...By the grace of God I am not dead yet, nor have I lost my senses. On the contrary, I have been a lawyer, I have been a bishop, and I have had to deal with such matters many times. Why then, when I am Rector Major, am I not to be consulted?
>
> For the sake of charity, tell me what you are doing and what you propose to do. As bishop and lawyer, I have advised in a thousand matters but now, in your opinion, I am incapable of anything....[11]

While Alphonsus pictured to himself the possible state of affairs of the houses of the Papal States, Father Majone, to whom he had entrusted the negotiations for royal approbation, labored in Naples. After reading several of his reports which spoke encouragingly of the improved climate of opinion toward their cause, Alphonsus answered:

Things seem to be going well now. Let us permit Our
Lord to act. He has worked miracles in these persecutions of ours, as your Reverence knows well, and I am
certain that He will not permit His work to be destroyed....
I am feeling much worse but I shall die content if I am
able, by the grace of God and the protection of Mary, to
see the end of this restlessness before my death.[12]

For most of his adult life Alphonsus had labored to protect
the rule of his Congregation. He had grown old living out every
one of its articles and passionately implored his brethren over and
over to love it as he did. Several times in the past he had fought
with vital determination attempts to mitigate in various ways the
constitutions that bound together the Congregation of the Most
Holy Redeemer. Fresh perils only served to strengthen his resolve
to permit nothing to alter a document he considered the life of his
Institute.

In the month of August, 1779, Matthew Testa, Grand Almoner at the court in Naples, expressed his belief that the king
might respond favorably to a renewed request for royal approbation of this cherished rule. All that was required, he assured the
aged rector major, would be the removal of all provisions contrary to previous royal decrees. Thinking that the articles referred
to applied only to the acquisition and retention of property,
Alphonsus decided to stake everything on a final effort at the royal
approval of the rule so necessary to the continued existence of the
Congregation.

Two delegates were chosen by the consultors to represent their
interest in Naples: Father Majone, who was already in Naples on
community business, and Father Cimino. The instructions the old
man gave the two delegates were simple: they were not to compromise any important articles of the rule. Their authority, then,
covered only those portions of the rule dealing with the financial
affairs of the Congregation.

When Majone and Cimino reached Naples and handed the
text of the rule to Monsignor Testa, their hopes began to crumple.
One by one Testa struck out every provision of the rule that was
opposed to previous royal decrees. Provisions for vows, the oath

of perseverance, the authority of the rector major, the convocation of general chapters: all these and more were deleted from the text of the rule. Without informing their fellow consultors and without consulting Alphonsus himself, Majone and Cimino attempted negotiations on their own.

Rumor soon reached various houses of what was happening at Naples. Many, alarmed at the possibilities presented by the situation, wrote to Alphonsus repeating the rumors that had come to them and asking for clarification. The following response to Don Bartolomeo Corrado at Ciorani (September 4, 1779) is typical of the many replies he sent to those who were alarmed. He could not know that the rumors he dismissed as incredulous were indeed true.

> My dear Don Bartolomeo:
>
> I hear that some are saying that I want to devise a different rule than that which now binds us. How could anyone ever suspect me of this since I have always been most careful to preserve that rule. I have always governed the Congregation in accordance with that rule and I will try with all my strength until my last breath to prevent even the slightest change.[13]

When Corrado insisted again that several reliable sources had informed him that the rule *was* being changed, and changed substantially, Alphonsus again replied (December 15, 1779):

> I have received your letter and thought about every word. I do not think that you can possibly believe that I am deceiving you, or that I am lying, or that I am so senile that I could permit anything to be changed in the rule. I say no more. If I am not to be believed, what can I say? My sins are at fault. It gives me great pain to hear these things. I repeat: You can be sure, on my conscience, that there is nothing against the rule or against the strict observance of the common life. If you do not believe me, I can do nothing.[14]

In spite of the ill-informed assurances of Alphonsus, anxiety mounted throughout the houses of the Congregation and every seam of apparent unity strained to the breaking point. Writing to Father Tannoia, Rector of Iliceto (and later the first biographer of the saint) on December 17, 1779, he pleaded:

> My Don Antonio,
> The devil is trying to shatter the Congregation. Father Cimino and the rest think that your presence will help matters, so I beg you to come at once...the devil has planted the suspicion, even at Iliceto, that Father Majone and Father Cimino want to change the rule and do away with community life. Tell everyone that it is a complete lie. How could I ever, in conscience, permit life to be taken away, or the rule to be altered?[15]

As greater unrest moved throughout the houses of the Congregation, Alphonsus wrote to Majone in Naples demanding an answer to the charges made against him by other members. Afraid to face Alphonsus with the truth, and knowing he had already come too far to back away from the negotiations initiated, Majone phrased his answer in misleading terms, hoping to postpone disaster. He told his rector major that he would never be guilty of harming the Congregation or of destroying community life. He did not, in fact, believe that the changes, of which he knew, would have the effect many feared. Alphonsus was satisfied.

But Majone knew that sooner or later he would have to face the old man, since his signature was required to validate the final draft of the petition to the king. The risk of rejection was great, but the slim possibility existed that Alphonsus would sign the document without realizing its contents. While he was not senile by any means, he was almost blind. His hearing was so weak that even when someone read a letter or document to him, he tired easily from the strain of simply listening intensely to someone else's voice.

In September 1779, Father Majone arrived at Pagani with a carefully prepared copy of the brief, handwritten in the smallest possible script. The manuscript was further complicated by numerous marginal notes and additions to the text. He felt fairly confident that Alphonsus would be unable to read the document himself. His hopes were realized when Alphonsus, after making an effort to get through the first few pages, handed the text to his trusted friend and confessor, Father Villani, Vicar General of the Congregation. Having been previously convinced by Majone and Cimino that the changes were the only way to keep the Congregation in existence, and also persuaded by them that Alphonsus, if he realized the extent of the compromises would unwisely reject the changes and thus destroy the Congregation, Villani proceeded to read the rule to himself solemnly. After placing the rule on a nearby table, he gently assured the rector major that all the changes were minor and that they would not effect the present fervor of the Congregation. He advised Alphonsus to sign the document immediately, and Alphonsus did as he was advised.

The king signed the document of royal approbation on January 22, 1780. Yet Majone hesitated to reveal the news to the rest of the Congregation. On February 27 the *Regolamento* (rule of life approved by the king) finally arrived at Pagani in the hands of a messenger who was unaware of its contents. Since Alphonsus was considered too ill for undue excitement, the members asked Father Villani to open the package and read to them the newly approved rule. As article after article was read to the community, the priests gradually grasped the consequences of the document.

The following morning all crowded into the cell of the weary rector major to tell him of the disaster that had fallen upon the Congregation. Unwilling to respond to heresay, he asked for the copy of the official *Regolamento* so he could read it himself. Struggling through page after page, the old man began to sob uncontrollably: "I can't believe it," he said, "My Jesus, I trusted my confessor. If I cannot trust my confessor, whom can I trust? I have been betrayed."[16] The words cut into the heart of Villani who stood before him with his head bowed, and unable to speak.

The grief that overwhelmed Alphonsus seemed to bring on a coma, and he sat in his chair unable to move all morning. When Brother Francis brought him a little food later on in the afternoon, he looked up sadly and implored: "O my God, do not punish the innocent; punish me. I am guilty; I ruined your work." And with a great effort he pushed away the tray of food that was put before him. An official letter that arrived from Monsignor Testa a few days later only increased the anguish he struggled to cope with. It read, in part:

> You, as Founder and Superior General of the Institute, will be good enough to make known to all the subjects in my name that these statutes are to remain perpetually in force and that no changes will be permitted. All members of the Institute, present or future, whether priests or lay brothers, must submit themselves to it without opposition or contradiction. In order to accomplish this you will communicate this to all the local superiors commanding them to read it to their communities at their accustomed time and place of meeting, noting this fact in their archives for future reference and notifying me that they have executed the order.[17]

Alphonsus was helpless. To refuse to comply with the order would mean the swift and certain dissolution of the Congregation, yet to comply with the edict would also mean the slow destruction of a life's work through an impossible compromise of the rule. Hoping that others would see some loophole that in his anxiety he had missed, Alphonsus asked two trusted friends to come to Pagani, Father Tannoia and Father Corrado. Writing to Father Corrado at Ciorani, he confided:

> My Don Bartolomeo, I am in danger of insanity. The new *Regolamento* produced by Father Majone is completely against my wishes. All the young men here are in an uproar. I beg you to leave everything and come to me, if you do not want to see me lose my mind and die of a stroke.[18]

Their advice seemed to offer some sort of hope for the situation. They suggested that Alphonsus petition Monsignor Testa for an extension of the time allotted for putting the new rule into effect. In the meantime they also suggested petitioning Monsignor Testa to permit them to summon a special "assembly" (general chapters had been expressly forbidden) at Pagani to discuss the situation at the earliest possible date.

Father Majone was stripped of his office as consultor, but few gestures reveal the heart of Alphonsus more than the letter he addressed to Majone shortly after he had played the key role in breaking his heart (Monday of Holy Week, 1780):

> Embracing the feet of Jesus Christ, I write to you. I pray that you will do the same during these days in which Jesus Christ gave his life for our love.
> My Don Angelo,
> Let us forget the past and put all that has happened behind us. I beg you to go back to your house at Ciorani, or if that home does not please you choose one which will. Be sure that I, for my part, will love you as before. As for your reputation, leave it in my hands; I will constantly defend it both to our companions and to strangers. Let us then be at peace, I beg you by the wounds of Jesus Christ. I have no more to say. Meditate on this before the Blessed Sacrament, and then send me your answer. I beg you and pray Jesus Christ to fill you with His holy love and to make you all His own as He desires.[19]

Majone himself repented for having disobeyed the positive instructions of his rector major, but the damage had already been done. Monsignor Testa denied their appeal for suspension of the new rule and also refused permission for the convocation at Pagani. In desperation Alphonsus pleaded:

> If you refuse to listen to my sons, I myself will come to you, and if you refuse to listen to me, I will send a thousand letters to the Marquis de Marco and a thousand petitions to the King....[20]

Monsignor Testa relented slightly, agreeing to withhold enforcement of the new *Regolamento* until after the assembly at Pagani. Two representatives from each house of the Congregation were to examine the new rule and discuss what could be done.

Many throughout the Congregation, especially in the houses of the Papal States, listened to those who said that Alphonsus himself was responsible for the *Regolamento*. Yet several letters written during these dark days help us to see the truth. Writing to Father Fioccelli, Rector at Frosinone in the Papal States, he explained:

> Father Majone, by tampering with the old rule, has placed the whole Congregation on the brink of destruction....If we do not follow the original rule there will be in fact two Congregations, one in the Papal States and another in Naples. And if there are two Congregations, the Congregation of the Most Holy Redeemer will be destroyed....Few days are left for me. My desire is to leave the Congregation at peace, for Satan is the only one who gains from disquiet. But if God wills to call me in the midst of chaos, I have no other desire than to live and die doing the will of God.[21]

In spite of attempts by Alphonsus to reassure those in the Papal States, conditions worsened by the week. On February 23, 1780, Father de Paula had petitioned the presecretary of the Congregation of Bishops and Regulars, Don Philip Zuccari, for an investigation of the whole situation on behalf of the houses of the Papal States. The dating of the petition indicates that Alphonsus himself had not been informed of the *Regolamento* when de Paula, believing the rumors despite the reassurance of Alphonsus, pressed the case in Rome. When his petition was ignored, he settled down to think of a more effective course of action.

When official word arrived at Frosinone concerning the impending assembly at Pagani, Father Leggio, a friend of de Paula and equally eager to act at once, addressed the following letter to Rome:

> ...Sometime ago, through the efforts of a member of the Congregation, the houses in the kingdom of Naples altered our Rule by making changes which are completely opposed to the spirit of the rule and omitted entirely the vow which each of us takes to persevere in the Congrega-

tion until death. This has created a serious situation and what is worse, they are now thinking of introducing the *Regolamento,* which is already observed in the houses of the kingdom, into our houses in the Papal States. A general assembly has therefore been called.

...The innovation they hope to introduce is extremely displeasing to the petitioner who, therefore, has recourse to you so that you might command that in the houses of the Papal States, no changes must be accepted and that we must continue to follow the rule approved by Pope Benedict XIV.[22]

It is unfortunate that such an ill-advised document reached Rome before all the facts could be ascertained. The *Regolamento* had *not* been accepted by the Neopolitan houses nor had it been accepted by Alphonsus himself. In several letters to Frosinone, Alphonsus himself assured the fathers there, including de Paula and Leggio, that he loathed the changes negotiated by Father Majone and that the assembly at Pagani was being summoned to forestall putting its provisions into effect.

On May 12 the assembly finally met at Pagani. Fourteen delegates were to decide the fate of the Congregation, and Alphonsus himself was too ill to take an active role. Sessions were often stormy as each faction hurled bitter accusations at the other. Many felt that Alphonsus had betrayed his own Congregation; and he did nothing to deny the accusations.

When the meetings finally ended, the delegates decided to draw up another petition to Monsignor Testa at Naples, asking for certain modifications of the new rule. Actually, if the recommendations had been followed, the result would be a complete restoration of the old rule. Monsignor Testa rejected their proposals.

The alternatives seemed bleak indeed. The Congregation within the kingdom of Naples could choose to obey the *Regolamento* imposed by the government or it could cease to exist. A refuge was provided, it is true, by the houses in the Papal States. But the majority of vocations had come from Naples and much of their necessary income came from sources within the kingdom. Members were reluctant if not completely unwilling to leave the boundaries of the kingdom for what could be permanent exile. At no time did Alphonsus proposed to extend the *Regolamento* to the houses outside the kingdom, but fear that this could happen seems to have been a driving motive behind many of the actions that brought about a final split.

The situation seemed so grave and feelings toward those who allowed such a crisis to occur were so bitter that Alphonsus, thinking himself very much to blame, resigned his office as rector major. In accordance with the constitutions, his act of resignation also meant the resignations of all his consultors: Majone and Cimino, Villani and Mazzini, Cajone and Stephen Liguori (no relation). The assembly, not realizing that it could not technically and canonically function as a chapter, reelected Alphonsus as rector major and also elected a group of consultors to assist him: Villani, Tannoia, Corrado, Blasucci, Alexander de Meo, Pavone, and Father Costanzo. Alphonsus signed a document approving the election, which was one of the most serious mistakes of his life. According to the strict articles of the constitution, the election was completely invalid and, while perhaps justification can be found in the very nature of the crisis the Congregation was enduring, the fact remains that any opponent of the move had ample justification for proving his case.

As soon as the assembly had concluded, Father Francis de Paula, who had been a delegate but had refused to vote, returned to his house at Frosinone. Almost immediately he sent a second letter to the Congregation of Bishops and Regulars at Rome which precipitated the split of the Congregation. He said in part:

> ...The priest Francis de Paula...humbly makes known the fact that some of the Fathers living in the houses of the kingdom have met in a special assembly with their Superior General, Msgr. Liguori, after accepting new regulations completely opposed to the Rule, have elected new officials according to these regulations. The petitioner believes that the Superior General, having abandoned the original rule and having embraced the new regulations, has CEASED TO BE SUPERIOR GENERAL OF THE HOUSES SUBJECT TO THE AUTHORITY OF THE

POPE, AND WITH HIM THE WHOLE BODY OF CONSULTORS. Their offices are therefore vacant, and we must convoke a General Chapter for the canonical election provided for in our Rule. But since there is no one in authority to convoke the Chapter, the petitioner and many others finds himself in great confusion. He, therefore, begs your Eminence in the name of all to instruct them as to what to do, unless the Sacred Congregation sees fit to appoint by its authority one of the Fathers President who might convoke a General Chapter and govern the Congregation provisionally until it can meet.[23]

Within a few days, at the suggestion of de Paula and Leggio, the rectors of the other houses outside the kingdom had also sent letters to the Sacred Congregation, protesting the actions of the assembly and pledging their obedience to the original rule.

De Paula had also written to Father Blasucci in Sicily urging him to aid them in their attempt at independence. Blasucci's response (July 30, 1780) reveals his deep loyalty to Alphonsus, as well as his profound common sense. His analysis of the situation is one of the few objective ones recorded during the period.

My dearest brother,

I have received your letter. Even if I have not been fully informed of current events, they are certainly not news to me. I do not understand why you needed to petition His Holiness in the name of the houses of the Papal States so that he might order you to observe the rule approved by Benedict XIV, and not the new royal ordinances enforceable only in the four houses within the kingdom. It has not occurred to the King to try to govern those outside his kingdom.

Your petition, then, has only served to discredit the Neopolitan portions of the Congregation in Rome, as if it were degenerate, and even to discredit the houses in the Papal States, since they are consequently members of an unstable community.

It has also helped to imprudently provoke the anger of the King who, sooner or later, will be informed of your actions and might close the houses in the kingdom; or at least forbid any connection between the two parts of the Congregation. If this happens your houses will also die. Such an ill-considered step does not seem to me to be an impulse of true zeal.

I read with horror in your letter: "We will elect a new Rector Major in September since Msgr. Liguori has forfeited this dignity. I have never considered a person led by the Spirit of God who is the enemy of unity."

Dear Brother, I take the liberty of censuring this choleric outburst which comes from a heart not altogether a stranger to secret ambitions. I am your brother.…Love to be in the house, nothing in the Congregation, superior of yourself, alone before God alone great by humility. Remember why you entered the Institute. Sooner or later God will heal our wounds and the Congregation, in spite of hell, will always be a Congregation. It displeases me that you want a place in the history of the schism like Jeroboam among the Israelites. Do not make yourself leader of four ill-advised superiors who are withdrawing themselves from the obedience to the holy old man, Msgr. Liguori, created by the Pope Rector Major for life.

Dear Brother, do not be offended by my freedom, for I love you and I write with love, and am your senior in age being in my fifty-eighth year. For my consolation, I hope to hear from you soon so that there may be one spirit and one love between us.[24]

Blasucci also sent a copy of this letter to Alphonsus. Three weeks later Alphonsus sent him the following reply:

My dear Peter-Paul: I really understand that it would be difficult for you to come to Naples but when one is in danger of drowning he takes any remedy he can find. I think it is important that you come to Naples. Your letter will help very much but I still see the Congregation al-

most destroyed. Mine is a living death. I can call it nothing else.

...Your Reverence should come to Naples and visit all
our houses. I am a poor cripple and can scarcely breathe.
Breath fails me more every day.[25]

Father Blasucci did not go to Naples. Before arrangements
could be made for his departure it was too late to be of any use.
Within a few weeks, without consulting Alphonsus, Father Lupoli,
rector of the house of studies at Iliceto, and all twelve seminarians
moved to Beneventum in the Papal States.

On August 4, 1780, the following letter from the Sacred Congregation came to the Archbishop of Beneventum and the Bishop
of Veroli in the Papal States:

> ...Your Lordship will be so good as to make known to
> the two houses of your diocese that, pending an investi-
> gation of the alleged invalidity of the elections made in
> the recent assembly, they are not to execute any order
> coming from the superiors elected by that assembly....
> Moreover, your Lordship will be so good as to ascertain
> from the older members whether there are objections to
> appointing Father de Paula as temporary superior.[26]

On September 22, 1780, the pope signed a provisional decree
that in effect excluded Alphonsus from his own Congregation.
The copy that was forwarded to Father de Paula stated:

> His Holiness, wishing to provide legitimate superiors
> for the houses of the Congregation of the Most Holy Re-
> deemer in the diocese of Veroli and the diocese of
> Beneventum...has graciously deigned to appoint your
> Reverence the President of their houses, giving you all the
> necessary faculties so that you may preside over the gov-
> ernment of these houses and their members according to
> the Rules and Constitutions of the Congregation of the
> Most Holy Redeemer, approved by Pope Benedict XIV, in
> place of those who, being higher superiors of the Congre-

gation, have adopted a new system essentially different and have deserted the Institute in which they were professed, and have *truly ceased to be members of the Congregation or to enjoy any of the privileges and graces granted to it by the Holy See....*[27]

When Father Villani told Alphonsus what had happened he could do little more than weep. As the tears streamed down his face silently he said, almost inaudibly: "I will only what God wills. His grace is enough for me." In spite of his resignation, the news brought on one of the most severe attacks of depression he had ever experienced. The more he prayed the more he felt tempted to despair. Over and over he begged his companions: "Help me. God has abandoned the Congregation because of my sins. Help me; I don't want to offend God."

The decree had come as a shock even to those in the Papal States who had been responsible for the drastic action taken by the Holy See. Half the Congregation was now forbidden to give missions or carry on in any way the work of the community. The strongest half had been silenced. What would they do now? De Paula himself, writing to Tannoia soon after word had reached Frosinone, insisted:

...I assure you that I have never intended to do anything but to uphold the Congregation which I saw going to ruin. You can assure Monsignore, our Father, and everyone else of this. Even if the Pope has appointed me President and interim superior of the four houses of the Pontifical States, I will not rest until Msgr. Liguori is restored as our superior and peace comes once again to our Congregation in the eyes of Rome....If people doubt my sincerity, have Father Blasucci come from Sicily as soon as possible and in November we will go to Rome together and beg the Pope to help us to repair the wound....I profess myself the most obedient son of the Monsignore, our Father, in all that he shall command me to do and I feel a true obligation on me to support him and the Congregation he has founded.[28]

In spite of all the insistence of good will that pours forth from every side during these trying days, it is apparent that words are much cheaper than actions. For the more each side insisted on its desire for union, the more it seemed to work toward a deeper separation.

The suffering of Alphonsus became intense. For most of his adult life he had vowed to live a life of poverty, celibacy, and obedience. If he was no longer recognized as a legitimate member of the Congregation, what was he to do? His conscience became tormented, especially on the subject of poverty. In a letter to Father Corrado (June 28, 1781) he reveals his struggles.

> Will your Reverence make known to the Pope that since I am bound to my old rule to observe my vow of poverty, I should depend on the dispensations of the Superior of the Congregation in special cases of doubt. But now I have no superior and I am in a terrible state of torment, and the devil is tempting me to despair. I do not want to offend God in the smallest way and so I will *not* despair, but I beg your Reverence to consult the Pope privately and to reveal my agitation to him, since these doubts and scruples are a state of continual death. I beg you to ask the Pope's permission for me to depend on my confessor's judgment when in doubt and so free me from my present state of confusion.[29]

When Father Corrado secured the necessary permission from the Grand Penitentary, the conscience of Alphonsus fixed itself on a second point. Although chained to his cell by so many physical afflictions that it would be difficult to list them all here, he felt somehow bound to travel to the Papal States where he could once more live in the midst of a community that was canonically accepted. He did not rest until he had written to Father de Paula, asking him to assign him to any house he wished. Father de Paula, aware of the wretched condition of Alphonsus, suggested that it was God's will that he remain at Pagani.

Most of the time Alphonsus accepted the state of his beloved Congregation with a spirit of sincere and complete resignation.

But some of the time his mind wandered and he would try to piece the sorrows together logically. They did not seem to fit. *"We obey the original rule; we have taken vows and we keep them. Why don't we belong to the Congregation? Why are we outside?"*[30] All anyone could say to him at times like this was to answer him that somehow he *did* belong to the Congregation but they did not describe how.

A large number of the Neopolitan fathers, realizing the situation the Papal decree placed them in, crossed the frontiers of the kingdom and permanently attached themselves to the houses of the Papal States. Other members of the community, tormented by the unrest that had shaken the Congregation and unsure of the future, chose to return to their homes. Among them were the very men who had created the situation that had torn the community in two: Father Majone and Father Cimino.

Some bishops, misunderstanding the judgment of the Sacred Congregation, treated the Neopolitan fathers as though they were guilty of formal heresy. Monsignor Angelo Zucchari, for example, Bishop of Capuccio, replying to the request of a rural district for Redemptorist missionaries, stated:

Certainly, provided that you accept those from the Papal States, true sons of the Church, recognized as such by the Pope and true sons of the most Holy Redeemer. The "Cioranists" of the kingdom, having acted in opposition to the authority of the Church, have rightly been denied all the privileges that the Holy See had granted to them. May the Lord enlighten them and draw them from the terrible condition which they share with all those who refuse obedience to the Vicar of Christ.[31]

The more his friends tried to console him in this trial, the more Alphonsus resisted consolation. *"Do not call me founder,"* he told a young priest one day; *"Call me a miserable sinner."*[32] It is God who has founded the Congregation. I have been but a useless instrument in His hand...."

By the autumn of 1784 the few shreds of an apostolate that he had managed to retain were withdrawn. He was no longer able to sustain correspondence with a number of religious he had directed for years; even his letters to Brianna Carafa ceased in this year. The brief daily contact he sometimes enjoyed with the people when he went for his afternoon drive stopped when his doctors forbade it due to the development of a new hernia which was aggravated by the jolts of the springless carriage. The extent of his exercises became a brief ride in his wheelchair up and down the corridors of the top floor of the monastery. This, then, became the scope of his world.

Since he no longer needed the horses that once faithfully drew his carriage, he ordered that they be sold so that the money might be given to the poor. His letter of instructions on the matter to Brother Michael might strike us today as a little too honest!

> You will let any interested buyer know that one of them has a sore mouth and cannot chew oats or straw, and that the older of the two has fits of lunacy and throws himself on the ground from time to time. To make him rise you must pull his ears. Explain all this clearly so that my conscience will be at peace.[33]

Needless to say, the price obtained for the unfortunate animals suffered considerably from the instructions for sale.

As his internal torment became more intense, Alphonsus felt that even his brief tours in a wheelchair were against charity. After all, a brother had to spend his time and energy in pushing him and the noise made by the revolving wheels could easily disturb those at prayer. Only his confessor could persuade him to continue.

By November of 1785 Alphonsus could no longer say Mass at all, yet he consoled himself with the privilege of attending the Mass of Father Garzilli in the chapel next to his cell. Even though his whole body was tormented with pain and the wound in his chest caused by the pressure of his twisted neck had freshly reopened several times, he confessed sincerely: *"I have stopped doing penance. The saints did not live this way."*[34]

As his days grew longer and longer and his ability to sleep even a few hours a night waned, Alphonsus asked Brother Francis to read the lives and writings of Saint Teresa and Saint Francis de Sales over and over to him. These two saints had profoundly influenced the course of his life; now they would help him to face death with courage and peace. But peace would not come cheaply to a man who was so poor.

For almost a year and a half the most severe temptations to despair tormented his soul, driving him at times to what he thought was the brink of hell. Scruples battered his conscience until all he could do was grope in the darkness for someone else's hand to show him the way. *"I turn to God,"* he said one day in anguish, *"but in answer to every word I pray a voice tells me that God is rejecting my prayer. I cry out: 'My Jesus I love you' and the voice responds: 'You are lying.'"* [35] Later, thinking about his inactive state, he would moan: *"I do not say Mass, I do not recite my office, I do not do a single good work; my senses are undisciplined, and I eat like an animal. I cannot understand how God still endures me."* [36] His only consolation rested in his complete obedience to his confessor who helped him rise above these frequent attacks of scruples. But even in this area he sometimes admitted: *"My mind does not want to obey. Lord grant me the strength to conquer myself and to submit."* [37]

Doubts poured into his soul about every truth of the faith that he had ever accepted. In the midst of them, all he could say in reply was: *"O Lord, yes, I do believe, and I want to live and die a child of the Church."* [38] Violent temptations against purity, humility, and poverty tormented him night and day, leaving the old man no apparent peace. Father Volpicelli, passing him in the hall one day, heard him accusing himself of having abandoned all his religious obligations.

"But Monsignore," said the priest trying to reassure him, "you can satisfy all your obligations with an ardent act of love."

"With an ardent act of love," replied Alphonsus, and then after a long and tormented pause, he said simply: *"Teach me how to make an act of love."* [39]

At least eighteen months of the saint's life was spent in these torments until the last storm finally passed in the spring of 1787. The little strength that remained to him had been drained by his psychological condition, and each day saw him a little nearer to death. His throat became so sore that it became painful to swallow food in any form; even soup seemed sometimes to have the consistency of thorns.

By the end of July everyone knew that the end was not far off. Alphonsus would lapse into a coma that would last for days and then would recover consciousness for a few hours at most. About ten o'clock on July 25 he received the Holy Eucharist, praying in a barely audible voice, *"My Jesus, My Jesus, never leave me again."*[40] His wish was granted at last as the temptations that had assailed him seemed to slip from him like great weights.

On August 1, 1787, Alphonsus gently fell asleep in Jesus. A picture of Mary and a crucifix were resting peacefully on his chest and the noon Angelus bell he loved so much was ringing insistently through the cloisters. He had lived and labored for ninety years in the Church of Christ. He had been a missionary, priest, lawyer, founder, and bishop. He struggled and conquered, but he had also struggled and lost.

Notes

CHAPTER 1

1. "Nacque egli nel casino di Marianella vicino alla città di Napoli feudo di sua. Famiglia ai 27 Settembre 1696, e poco. Dopo nella festa di S. Michele Archangelo. Ricevete il Battesimo nella chiesa Parocchiale de Vergini." Piere Luigi Rispoli, *Vita del B. Alfonso Maria de Liguori* (Napoli: Tipografia Sangiacomo, 1834), p. 7. "La sua Famiglia si antica che componevani l'ordine intiero della noblità Napoletana. La Signoria de Liguori s'incontra nell 1190. Marco Liguori in quell' epoca, fu firmato da lui." Gregorio, Capone, Freda, Toglia, *Sant' Alfonso de Liguori: Contributi Bio-Bibliografi* (Varese: La Tipografia Varese, 1940), p. 35.

2. "Quanto di Bene riconosco in me nella mia Fanciulezza, dirà, e se non Hofatta del male, di tutto son debitore alle sollecitudini di mia madre." Quoted in Oreste Gregorio, "Reveduta Sulle Richerche Alfonsiane," *Sant' Alfonso de Liguori* edited by Alfonso Salvini (Bari: Edizioni Paoli, 1940), p. 9.

"La madre de Alfonso fu D. Anna Caterina Cavalieri, dama discendente da nobilissima famiglia de brindisi era sorella del celebre servio di dio emilio gia como Cavilere." Piere Luigi Rispoli. *Vita del B. Alfonso Maria de Liguori*, p. 8.

3. "It is barely half a century since growing attention has been given by historians to the extremely important development which scalled 'Jansenist' tendencies experienced during the eighteenth century, even inside the Sacred College, the high prelature and the religious orders mainly the Oratory and the Pious Schools."

Maurice Vaussard, *Daily Life in Eighteenth Century Italy*, tr. by Michael Heron (London: George Allen and Unwin, 1962), p. 79.

4. Jean Jacques Olier, *Catechisme Chretien*, Part I, L. 20.

5. Saint Alphonsus Liguori, "A Christian's Rule of Life," *Considerations on the Eternal Truths*, translated from the Italian and edited by Eugene Grimm (Brooklyn: Redemptorist Fathers, 1926), pp. 413-465.

6. "Egli lo fece entrape in età dieci anni, nella Congregatione di Giovani nobili, diretti, dà Padri dell' Oratorio."

Piere Luigi Rispoli, *Vita del B. Alfonso Maria de Liguori*, p. 12.

7. "Non mancò ad Alfonso l'erudizione detle umane lettere, nella Cosmografia, Geografia Istoria, mitologiá chronologia, ed anche l'idioma Latino, Greco, e Francese."

Piere Luigi Rispoli, *Vita del B. Alfonso Maria de Liguori*, p. 12.

8. "Nell eta di anni tredici eseguiva mirabilmente le composizioni difficili im musica. Se ne avvalse poi pel bene delle anime. Compose un duetto tra l'anima, e Gesu appasionata, che se cantò in Napoti nella chiese detle Trinita de' Pellegrini prima della sua Predica, e commosee tutta la numerosa Udienza. Si applico con tanto impegno alta musica, che disse, guardiando it sue cembalo in Nocera de'Pagani, ove con servasi: 'Pazzo che sono stato in averci perduto tanto tempo, ma dovea ubbidure a mio Padre'."

Piere Luigi Rispoli, *Vita del B. Alfonso Maria de Liguori*, p. 12.

9. "During the 230 years under Spanish and German rule, the history of Naples furnishes an example of everything a country and a government should not be....The Departments of Justice were in dire confusion. One power after another had made new laws without repealing the old or properly instituting new codes. Different parts of the Kingdom were under different laws."

Clara Clement Waters, *Naples: The City of Parthenope and Its Environs* (Boston: Estes and Lauriat, 1894), p. 136.

10. Antoine-Marie Tannoia, *Mémoires Sur la Vie et la Congrégation de S. Alphonse-Maria de Liguori* (Paris: Gaume Freres 1842), Volume I, p. 15.

11. Austin Berthe, *Life of Saint Alphonsus de Liguori Bishop and Doctor of the Church*, translated and edited by Harold Castle (St. Louis: B. Herder, 1906), Volume I, p. 8.

12. Piere Luigi Rispoli, *Vita del B. Alfonso Maria de Liguori.*

13. "It is said that in 1734 eleven methods of legislation actually existed in this peninsula, while the courts were filled with corrupt officials and lawyers."

Clara Clement Waters, *Naples, The City of Parthenope and Its Environs*, p. 136.

14. "Noblemen went to the performances more to be seen and to see, to gamble and pay court to the ladies than to thrill on hearing what was often exquisite music."

Maurice Vassary, *Daily Life in Eighteenth Century Italy* (London: George Allen and Unwin, 1962), p. 159.

15. Raimundo Tellería, *San Alfonso Mariá de Liguori, Fundador, Obispo Y Doctor* (Madrid: Editorial el Perpetuo Socorro, 1950), Tomo I, p. 93.

16. Austin Berthe, *Life of Saint Alphonsus de Liguori Bishop and Doctor of the Church,* Volume I, p. 12.

17. Raimundo Tellería, *San Alfonso Mariá de Liguori, Fundador, Obispo Y Doctor,* Tomo I, p. 72.

18. Oreste Gregorio, Domenico Capone, Ambrogio Freda, and Vincenzo Toglia, "S. Alfonso e D. Teresina DeLiguori," *Sant' Alfonso de Liguori: Contributi Bio-Bibliografi* (Varese: La Tipografia Varese, 1940), pp. 56-57.

"L'idea del fidazamento di Alfonso con Teresina concepita da P. Giuseppe suini nel 1711 con la nascita di D. Cesare, che secondo ogni previsione sarebbe divenuto l'erede dei beni principeschi. Ció che con una abitudine ormai inveterata si suole narrare dopo la nascita di lui esoda dai confini della storia, poichè poggia sopra un fondamento dimonstrato falso in radice...Questa e la storia genuina; il resto è leggenda."

19. Austin Berthe, *Life of Saint Alphonsus de Liguori Bishop and Doctor of the Church,* V. I, p. 18.

20. Austin Berthe, V. I, p. 20.

21. Austin Berthe, V. I, p. 22.

22. J. T. Mullock, *The Life of Saint Alphonsus M. Liguori Bishop of St. Agatha and Founder of the Congregation of the Most Holy Redeemer* (New York: P. J. Kenedy, 1-96), p. 52.

23. "The complicated system of customary rights and legislation applied by a dozen successive governments—Roman, Byzantine, Angevin, Aragonese, and Spanish—had made Neopolitan law into such a jungle that it offered the best atmosphere for roguery...certain cases lasted for centuries."

Maurill Vaussary, *Daily Life in Eighteenth Century Italy,* p. 84.

24. "Un avvocato che perde una causa per propria negligenza si carica dell'obbligazione di risarchire il cliente di ogni danno."

Alfonso Salvini, *Sant'Alfonso de Liguori* (Bari: Edizioni Paolini, 1940), p. 15.

25. Austin Berthe, *Life of Saint Alphonsus de Liguori Bishop and Doctor of the Church,* V. I. p. 23.

26. Austin Berthe, p. 25.

27. Antoine-Marie Tannoia, *Mémoires sur la Vie et la Congrégation de S. Alphonse-Maria de Liguori,* V. I, p. 46.

28. Antoine-Marie Tannoia, V. I, p. 41.

29. On April 27, many years later, while sharing recreation with younger members of his Congregation, Alphonsus announced softly: "This is the anniversary of my conversion." After much prompting, Alphonsus then shared with them the experience that is briefly retold here.
Antoine-Marie Tannoia, V. I, p. 42.

30. Antoine-Marie Tannoia, V. I, p. 44.

31. Raimundo Tellería, *San Alfonso Mariá de Liguori, Fundador, Obispo Y Doctor,* Tomo I, p. 95.

32. Raimundo Tellería, Tomo I, p. 95.

33. Raimundo Tellería, Tomo I, p. 96.

34. Raimundo Tellería, Tomo I, p. 96.

35. Austin Berthe, *Life of Saint Alphonsus de Liguori Bishop and Doctor of the Church,* V. I, p. 30.

36. Austin Berthe, V. I, p. 30.

37. Austin Berthe, V. I, p. 31.

CHAPTER 2

1. Austin Berthe, *Life of Saint Alphonsus de Liguori Bishop and Doctor of the Church,* V. I, p. 32.

2. "Convinced that the Holy Scriptures should be a priest's favorite book, he never passed a day without this divine study, whose inner meaning his constant prayer helped him to penetrate."
Austin Berthe, V. I, p. 33.

3. "Ha nombrado a Santa Teresa, su maestra y confidente. Más tarde la declará Patrona especial de las almas probadas en el crisol de augustias espiratuales. Ahor la regalo con el título de 'segundo da mama,' y no se saciaba de apellidarla Santa mia."
Raimundo Tellería, *San Alfonso Maria de Liguori, Fundador, Obispo Y Doctor,* Tomo I, p. 142.

4. Austin Berthe, *Life of Saint Alphonsus de Liguori Bishop and Doctor of the Church,* V. I, p. 35.

5. Antoine-Marie Tannoia, *Mémoires sur la Vie et la Congrégation de S. Alphonse-Maria de Liguori,* V. 1, p. 51.

6. Antoine-Marie Tannoia, V. I, p. 55.

7. Antoine-Marie Tannoia, V. I, p. 55-56.

8. "What universal good would flow from Sunday sermons if preachers always spoke to the people in plain and simple language. At Naples...the churches are filled with great numbers of faithful, especially the poor. How fruitful would the sermons preached in these churches be if the ministers adopted a popular style....But the style is generally high and flowery, and so they are but little understood by the people."
St. Alphonsus de Liguori, "Letter to a Religious," *Preaching,* translated from the Italian and edited by Eugene Grimm (New York: Benziger Brothers, 1889), p. 37.

9. St. Alphonsus de Liguori, *Preparation for Death; or Considerations on the Eternal Truths,* translated from the Italian and edited by Eugene Grimm (St. Louis: Redemptorist Fathers, 1926).

10. Raimundo Tellería, *San Alfonso Maria de Liguori, Fundador, Obispo Y Doctor,* Tomo I, p. 116.

11. Austin Berthe tells us Alphonsus composed this short prayer for his own use. Quoted in: Austin Berthe, *Life of Saint Alphonsus de Liguori Bishop and Doctor of the Church,* V. I, p. 42.

12. St. Alphonsus Liguori, "Letter to a Religious on the Manner of Preaching with Apostolic Simplicity." *Preaching,* p. 39.

13. Quoted in Austin Berthe, *Life of Saint Alphonsus de Liguori Bishop and Doctor of the Church,* V. I, p. 46.

14. Quoted in Austin Berthe, V. I, p. 46.

15. Antoine-Marie Tannoia, *Mémoires sur la Vie et la Congrégation de S. Alphonse-Maria de Liguori,* V. I, pp. 77-80.

16. Antoine-Marie Tannoia, V. I, pp. 81-82.

17. Antoine-Marie Tannoia, V. I, p. 82.

18. Austin Berthe, *Life of Saint Alphonsus de Liguori Bishop and Doctor of the Church,* V. I, p. 51.

32-I—SISTERS

19. Raimundo Tellería, *San Alfonso Maria de Liguori, Fundador, Obispo Y Doctor,* Tomo I, p. 127.

20. Raimundo Tellería, Tomo I, pp.127-128.

21. Antoine-Marie Tannoia, V. I, p. 92.

22. Antoine-Marie Tannoia V. I, p. 92.

23. This anecdote, taken from "Lettres ad un Vescovo...sulle Misioni" appears as a footnote in Raimundo Tellería, Tomo I, p. 33, n. 58.

24. Austin Berthe, V. I, p. 59.

CHAPTER 3

1. Raimundo Tellería, *San Alfonso Maria de Liguori, Fundador, Obispo Y Doctor* (Madrid: Editorial El Perpetuo Socorro, 1950) Tomo I, p. 148.

2. Raimundo Tellería, Tomo I, p. 152.

3. Raimundo Tellería, Tomo I, p. 151.

4. Raimundo Tellería, Tomo I, p. 152.

5. *Una Grande Mistica del '700: Autobiografia de la Ven. le Madre Sr. Maria Celeste Crostarosa*, edited by P. Benedetto D'Orazio (Frosinone: Abbazia di Casamari, 1965), Introduction.

6. *Autobiografia de la Ven. le Madre Sr. Maria Celeste Crostarosa*, p. 133.

7. Austin Berthe, *Life of Saint Alphonsus de Liguori*, V. I, p. 66.

8. Austin Berthe, V. I, p. 66.

9. Falcoia shared this early experience with Cesare Sportelli who served him as personal secretary for some time. Raimundo Tellería, Tomo I, p. 178.

10. Maur. de Meulemeester, *Histoire Sommaire de la Congregation du T. S. Rédempteur*, p. 25.

11. Raimundo Tellería, Tomo I, p. 178.

12. Raimundo Tellería, Tomo I, p. 155.

13. Austin Berthe, *Life of Saint Alphonsus de Liguori*, V. I, p. 68.

14. Austin Berthe, V. I, p. 68.

15. *Autobiografia de la Ven. le Madre Sr. Maria Celeste Crostarosa*, p. 176.

16. La declaracion de Sor Josefa Schiasano ex-Superiora y ca beza de la resistencia: 'Siendo así-dijo-no quiero contrariar la voluntad de Dios: soy la primera en abra zar la nueva Regla.' Quoted in Raimundo Telleria, Tomo I, p. 156.

17. Austin Berthe, V. I, p. 74.

18. St. Alphonsus Liguori, "To Mother Angiola del Cielo and to the Nuns of Scala," *Letters of Saint Alphonsus Maria de Liguori*, V. I, pp. 13-21.

19. St. Alphonsus Liguori, "To Mother Angiola del Cielo and to the Nuns of Scala," *Letters of Saint Alphonsus Maria de Liguori*, V. I, pp. 13-21.

20. Austin Berthe, V. I, p. 76.

21. Raimundo Tellería, Tomo I, p. 158.

22. Raimundo Tellería, Tomo I, p. 157.

23. Raimundo Tellería, Tomo I, p. 158.

24. Austin Berthe, V. I, p. 80.

25. Austin Berthe, V. I, p. 80.

26. *Autobiografia de la Ven. le Madre Sr. Maria Celeste Crostarosa*, pp. 186-187.

27. Austin Berthe, V. I, p. 83.
28. Raimundo Tellería, Tomo I, p. 148.
29. Austin Berthe, *Life of Saint Alphonsus de Liguori,* V. I, p. 152.
30. Austin Berthe, V. I, p. 85.
31. Austin Berthe, V. I, p. 65.
32. Austin Berthe, V. I, p. 65.
33. Austin Berthe, V. I, p. 88.
34. Austin Berthe, V. I, p. 70.
35. Austin Berthe, V. I, p. 71.
36. Raimundo Tellería, Tomo I, pp. 185-6.
37. Raimundo Tellería, Tomo I, p. 186.
38. "Confirmo y ratifico los preceptos que te ha dado el P. Pagano; no es preciso especificarlos; quiero que te atemperes a ellos para siempre....Te mando en virtud de santa obediencia. Si no los emplea no estoy obligado a ovedecerle por este voto." Quoted in Tellería, Tomo I, p. 201.

CHAPTER 4

1. Raimundo Tellería, *San Alfonso Maria de Liguori, Fundador, Obispo Y Doctor,* Tomo I, p. 191.
2. Raimundo Tellería, Tomo I, p. 196.
3. St. Alphonsus Liguori, "Notes on the Life of Vitus Curtius, Laybrother of the Congregation of the Most Holy Redeemer" *Miscellany* translated from the Italian and edited by Eugene Grimm (New York: Benziger Brothers, 1890), p. 278.
4. St. Alphonsus Liguori, "Notes on the Life of Vitus Curtius," *Miscellany,* p. 279.
5. Antoine-Marie Tannoia, *Memoires Sur la Vie et la Congregation de S. Alphonse-Maria de Liguori* V. I, p. 115.
6. Austin Berthe, V. I, p. 109.
7. Austin Berthe, V. I, p. 110.
8. Raimundo Tellería, Tomo I, p. 198.
9. Raimundo Tellería, Tomo I, p. 201.
10. St. Alphonsus Liguori, "Letter to Sister Maria Celeste Crostarosa, Nun of the Congregation of the Most Holy Savior of Scala." *Letters of Saint Alphonsus Maria de Liguori,* translated from the Italian and edited by Eugene Grimm (New York: Benziger Brothers, 1891), pp. 31-35.
11. Austin Berthe, *Life of Saint Alphonsus de Liguori,* V.1, pp. 120-121.

12. St. Alphonsus Liguori, "Letter to Sister Maria Celeste Crostarosa, Nun of the Congregation of the Most Holy Savior of Scala," *Letters of Saint Alphonsus Maria de Liguori,* translated from the Italian and edited by Eugene Grimm (New York: Benziger Brothers, 1891), pp. 35-48 Volume I.

13. Quoted in Austin Berthe, *Life of Saint Alphonsus de Liguori,* V. I, p. 124.

14. Quoted in Raimundo Tellería, *San Alfonso Maria de Liguori, Fundador, Obispo Y Doctor,* Tomo I, p. 313.

15. Quoted in Austin Berthe, *Life of Saint Alponsus de Liguori,* V. I, pp. 124-5.

16. Quoted in Austin Berthe, V. I, p. 125.

17. Raimundo Tellería, *San Alfonso Maria de Liguori, Fundador, Obispo Y Doctor,* Tomo I, p. 214.

18. Raimundo Tellería, Tomo I, p. 215.

19. Raimundo Tellería, Tomo I, p. 215.

20. Austin Berthe, *Life of Saint Alphonsus de Liguori,* V. I, p. 131.

21. Quoted in Austin Berthe, V. I, p. 133.

22. Lettre du 24 Janvier, 1734 au sujet de la vocation de Mazzini il raconte comment on s'y q'est pris chez les Pii Operarii pour faciliter sa propre entreé.

Maur. de Meulemeester, *Origines de la Congrégation du Très Saint-Redempteur; Etudes et Documents* (Louvain: Imprimerie S. Alphonse, 1957), p. 21.

23. "Priests engaged in parish work were comparatively few in number. It sometimes happened that a town with a population of several thousand had but two or three confessors. The great number of ecclesiastics exercised no active ministry. They lived in their parents' homes on the proceeds of some benefice."

Austin Berthe, *Life of Saint Alphonsus de Liguori,* V. I, p. 152.

24. "In the Kingdom of Naples, where it formed 2.5% of the population, the clergy collected a third of the revenues of the State. In the Duchy of Parma more than half and in Tuscany more than three-quarters of the territory was in the hands of ecclesiastical bodies during the first half of the century, before the reformist policy aimed at reducing the general spread of mortmain was applied...in Naples by Tannuci."

Maurice Vaussard, *Daily Life in Eighteenth Century Italy,* translated by Michael Heron (London: George Allen and Lenwin, 1962), pp. 74-75.

25. St. Alphonsus Liguori, "To Marquis Giuseppe Gioachino Montallegro," *Letters of Saint Alphonsus Liguori,* translated from the Italian and edited by Eugene Grimm, V. I, pp. 70-72.

26. Cantu. Stor. Univer., Book VI, chapter 29, quoted in Austin Berthe, *Life of Saint Alphonsus de Liguori*, V. I, p. 170.

27. Quoted in Austin Berthe, *Life of Saint Alphonsus de Liguori*, V. I, p. 170.

28. Quoted in Harold Acton, *The Bourbons of Naples: 1734-1825* (London: Methuen and Company, 1956), pp. 145-146.

29. Quoted in Harold Acton, pp. 120-121.

30. B. Croce, "Studi Sulla Vita Religiosa a Napoli nel '700," *Uomini e Cose Della Vecchia Italia*, V. XXI, (Bari, 1927).

31. Tannuci to his friend Viviani who had entertained the Grand Duke of Tuscany at dinner. Quoted in Harold Acton, *The Bourbons of Naples: 1734-1825* (London: Methuen and Company, 1956), p. 88.

32. "Religion had only an indirect bearing on the pretensions of the Neopolitan clergy. Their excessive number, their ever-increasing property, their immunity from taxation and their separate jurisdiction were some of the obvious causes of economic hardship in southern Italy." Harold Acton, *The Bourbons of Naples*, p. 31.

33. St. Alphonsus Liguori, "To Mgr. Tomasso Falcoia," *Letters of Saint Alphonsus Maria de Liguori*, V. I, p. 92.

34. Letter of January, 1738. Quoted in Austin Berthe, *Life of Saint Alphonsus de Liguori*, V. I, p. 193.

35. Testimony given at the process of canonization of St. Alphonsus by Father Villani. Quoted in Austin Berthe, V. I, p. 197.

36. It took over 200 years for the building at Ciorani to be completed, but enough donations were secured at this time to begin building the space seen as absolutely necessary. Austin Berthe, *Life of Saint Alphonsus de Liguori*, p. 198.

37. St. Alphonsus Liguori, "Notes on the Life of Father Januarius Sarnelli of the Congregation of the Most Holy Redeemer," *Miscellany*, translated from the Italian and edited by Eugene Grimm (New York: Benziger Brothers, 1890), p. 270.

38. Quoted in Austin Berthe, *Life of Saint Alphonsus de Liguori*, V. I, p. 181.

39. St. Alphonsus Liguori, "Notes on the Life of Father Januarius Sarnelli of the Congregation of the Most Holy Redeemer," p. 271.

40. Quoted in Austin Berthe, *Life of Saint Alphonsus de Liguori*, V. I, p. 206.

41. "Lettre de Sarnelli a Sant Alphonse, 18 Fevrier, 1741. Archives de la Postulatione C.S.S.R., Rome." Quoted in Maur. de Meulemeester *Orignes de la Congrégation du Très Saint-Redempteur: Etudes et Documents* (Louvain: Imprimerie S. Alphonse, 1957), 3.

42. Austin Berthe, *Life of Saint Alphonsus de Liguori,* V. I, p. 217.

43. Epistola "62, "Ad Villani"-25 Mart, 1743. *Epistolae Ven. Servi Dei Caesaris Sportelli* (Rome: Sumptibus Domus Generalitiae, 1937), pp. 85-86.

CHAPTER 5

1. Maur. de Meulemeester, *Origines de la Congrégation du Très Saint-Redempteur* (Louvain: Imprimerie S. Alphonse, 1957), p. 37.

2. Austin Berthe, *Life of Saint Alphonsus de Liguori Bishop and Doctor of the Church.* Translated and edited by Harold Castle (St. Louis: B. Herder, 1906), p. 233.

3. Raimundo Tellería, *San Alfonso Mariá de Liguori, Fundador, Obispo Y Doctor* (Madrid: Editorial el Perpetua Socorro, 1950), p. 346.

4. Raimundo Tellería, Tomo I, p. 364.

5. St. Alphonsus Liguori, "Notes on the Life of Father Sarnelli," *Miscellany,* edited by Eugene Grimm (New York: Benziger Brothers, 1890), pp. 271-272.

6. Raimundo Tellería, Tomo I, p. 362.

7. St. Alphonsus Liguori, "Notes on the Life of Father Sarnelli," *Miscellany, p.* 275.

8. Austin Berthe, *Life of Saint Alphonsus de Liguori,* V. I, p. 247.

9. Austin Berthe, V. I, p. 266.

10. St. Alphonsus Liguori, "To Father Xavier Rossi at Ciorani," December 19, 1744. *Letters of Saint Alphonsus Maria de Liguori,* translated from the Italian and edited by Eugene Grimm (New York: Benziger Brothers, 1891), V. I, pp. 137-140.

11. St. Alphonsus Liguori, "To Father Xavier Rossi at Ciorani," December 19, 1744, *Letters of Saint Alphonsus Maria de Liguori,* V. 1, pp. 140-143.

12. St. Alphonsus Liguori, "To Father Cesare Sportelli, Rector of the House at Pagani," *Letters of Saint Alphonsus Maria de Liguori,* V. I, p. 141.

13. Austin Berthe, V. I, p. 273.

14. Austin Berthe, V. I, p. 273.

15. Austin Berthe, V. I, p. 291.

16. Austin Berthe, V. I, p. 292.

17. Antoine-Marie Tannoia, *Mémoires Sur la Vie et la Congrégation de S. Alphonse-Maria de Liguori* (Paris: Gaume Freres, 1842).

18. "With a view to the studies which his professed chorists would have to make after the year of the novitiate, he undertook an important work on the whole range of matter comprised in moral theology. In this first attempt, which he published later on under the title of *Annotations to Busembaum,*...it

was therefore in the solitude of Iliceto, to help his young students, that he began to collect the material for that great theological work which has made him a Doctor of the Church." Quoted in Austin Berthe, V. I, pp. 295-296.

19. Austin Berthe, V. I, p. 297

20. Austin Berthe, V. I, p. 311.

21. Austin Berthe, V. I, p. 312.

22. St. Alphonsus Liguori, "To a General Consultor," August, 1747. *Letters of St. Alphonsus Maria de Liguori,* V. I, p. 186.

23. Austin Berthe, V. 1, pp. 315-316.

24. St. Alphonsus Liguori, "To the Soverign Pontiff Benedict XIV," *Letters of St. Alphonsus Maria de Liguori,* V. I, p. 199.

25. Austin Berthe, V. I, p. 329.

26. Full text quoted in the Appendix to Maur. de Meulemeester, *Origines de la Congregation du Très Saint-Redempteur* (Louvain: Imprimerie S. Alphonse, 1957), p. 277.

27. Full text quoted in Maur. de Meulemeester, p. 280.

28. Full text of letter quoted in the Appendix to Maur. de Meulemeester, p. 307.

29. Full text quoted in Maur. de Meulemeester, p. 307.

30. Full text of letter quoted in the Appendix to Maur. de Meulemeester, p. 308.

31. St. Alphonsus Liguori, "To Mother Angiola of Divine Love, a Carmelite at Capua," *Letters of Saint Alphonsus Maria de Liguori,* V. I, p. 287.

32. Austin Berthe, V. I, p. 331.

33. St. Alphonsus Liguori, "To the Fathers and the Brothers of the Congregation of the Most Holy Redeemer," *Letters of Saint Alphonsus Maria de Liguori,* V. I, pp. 331-342.

34. St. Alphonsus Liguori, "To the Novices of the House of Iliceto," January 28, 1762, *Letters of Saint Alphonsus Maria de Liguori,* V. I, pp. 597-600.

35. St. Alphonsus Liguori, "To the Fathers and Brothers of the Congregation of the Most Holy Redeemer," *Letters of Saint Alphonsus Maria de Liguori,* V. III, p. 29-35.

36. St. Alphonsus Liguori, "To the Fathers and Brothers of the Congregation," September 30, 1770, *Letters of Saint Alphonsus Maria de Liguori,* V. II, pp. 391-392.

37. Austin Berthe, V. I, p. 674.

38. Austin Berthe, V. I, p. 674.

39. Austin Berthe, V. I, p. 674.

40. St. Alphonsus Liguori, "To the Fathers and Brothers of the Congregation," *Letters of Saint Alphonsus Maria de Liguori,* V. II, pp. 489-494.

CHAPTER 6

1. The sciatic nerve in the leg had been accidently damaged some years before in the process of self-inflicted penance. The *promotor fidei* during the canonization process attempted to use this as an indication of imprudence. Raimundo Telleria, Tomo I, Chapter 10, p. 27.

2. Raimundo Tellería, Tomo I, p. 8.

3. Austin Berthe, *Life of Saint Alphonsus Maria de Liguori,* V. II, p. 3.

4. Austin Berthe, V. II, p. 3.

5. Austin Berthe, V. II, p. 3.

6. Raimundo Tellería, Tomo II, p. 2.

7. Raimundo Tellería, Tomo II, p. 13.

8. Raimundo Tellería, Tomo II, p. 13.

9. Raimundo Tellería, Tomo II, p. 14.

10. St. Alphonsus Liguori, "To His Brother Ercole," *Letters of Saint Alphonsus Maria de Liguori,* translated from the Italian and edited by Eugene Grimm, (New York: Benziger Brothers, 1891), V. II, pp. 3-5.

11. Quoted in Berthe, *Life of Saint Alphonsus de Liguori,* V. II, p. 11.

12. Quoted in Austin Berthe, V. II, p. 13.

13. Austin Berthe, V. II, p. 14.

14. Raimundo Tellería, Tomo II, p. 28.

15. Austin Berthe, V. II, p. 19.

16. Austin Berthe, V. II, p. 20.

17. Austin Berthe, V. II, p. 22.

18. Raimundo Tellería, Tomo II, p. 40.

19. Raimundo Tellería, Tomo II, p. 42.

20. Austin Berthe, V. II, p. 29.

21. St. Alphonsus de Liguori, "To the Sacred Congregation of the Council," *Letters of Saint Alphonsus Maria de Liguori: Special Correspondence,* translated from the Italian and edited by Thomas W. Mullaney (New York: Benziger Brothers, 1897), V. II.

22. The treasurer Modestino Criscuolo says: "the child died in the father's arms; the husband before the eyes of his wife, muttering one word, 'Bread! Bread!' People fed on wild herbs, and often on poisonous plants, which only accelerated death. Piles of corpses were removed by night so as not to frighten the living." From the Register of the Monte de Pietá of Avellino quoted from Salvator de Renzi, "Napoli nell anno 1764," found in Austin Berthe, V. II, p. 89.

23. Austin Berthe, V. II, p. 91.

24. St. Alphonsus Liguori, "To His Brother Don Ercole," *Letters of Saint Alphonsus Maria de Liguori*, V. II, p. 57.

25. St. Alphonsus Liguori, "To the Duke of Maddaloni," *Letters of Saint Alphonsus Maria de Liguori*, V. II, p. 63.

26. Raimundo Tellería, Tomo II, p. 124.

27. Austin Berthe, V. II, p. 97.

28. Austin Berthe, V. II, p. 98.

29. St. Alphonsus Liguori, "To Father Andrea Villani," *Letters of Saint Alphonsus Maria de Liguori*, V. II, p. 112.

30. St. Alphonsus Liguori, "To Father Andrea Villani," *Letters of Saint Alphonsus Maria de Liguori*, V. II, pp. 112-113

31. Austin Berthe, V. II, p. 173.

32. St. Alphonsus de Liguori, "To Father Andrea Villani," *Letters of Saint Alphonsus Maria de Liguori*, V. II, p. 128.

33. St. Alphonsus Liguori, "To Don Francesco Andrea Mostillo, Agent of the Duke of Maddaloni," *Letters of Saint Alphonsus Maria de Liguori*, V. II, p. 167.

34. St. Alphonsus Liguori, "To Sister Brianna Carafa in the Convent of St. Marcellino at Naples," July, 1768, *Letters of Saint Alphonsus Maria de Liguori*, V. II, p. 296.

35. St. Alphonsus Liguori, "To Father Andrea Villani," *Letters of Saint Alphonsus Maria de Liguori*, V. II, p. 295.

36. St. Alphonsus Liguori, "To Sister Brianna Carafa in the Convent of St. Marcellino at Naples," July, 1768, *Letters of Saint Alphonsus Maria de Liguori*, V. II, p. 296.

37. Raimundo Tellería, Tomo II, p. 352.

38. Quotation found in Raimundo Telleria, Tomo II, p. 353. It is also significant to note the following medical analysis: "Il Prof. Gennaro Goglia dell'Universita di Napoli in un accurato studio scientifico sul corpo del Santa (Roma 1958) rivela" 'I vari malanni, ma soprattutto l'artrosi lomvare e cervicale ebbero una notevole influenza sulla possibilita di muoversi ed opera.' Oreste Gregorio, *Monsignore Si Diverte* (Roma: Edizione Paoline), p. 188.

39. St. Alphonsus Liguori, "To Father Andrea Villani," Oct. 8, 1768, *Letters of Saint Alphonsus Maria de Liguori*, V. II, p. 307.

40. Austin Berthe, V. II, p. 262.

41. St. Alphonsus Liguori, "To Father Andrea Villani," *Letters of Saint Alphonsus Maria de Liguori*, V. III, pp. 62-63.

42. St. Alphonsus Liguori, "To Father Andrea Villani," March 9, 1775, *Letters of Saint Alphonsus Maria de Liguori*, V. III, p. 83.

43. St. Alphonsus Liguori, "To the Sovereign Pontiff Pius VI," *Letters of Saint Alphonsus Maria de Liguori,* V. III, pp. 102-103.

CHAPTER 7

1. Austin Berthe, V. II, p. 402.

2. "The blow that struck Tannuci has, they say, come from Vienna, from Rome and also from France. Such is the world," St. Alphonsus Liguori, "To Father Pietro Paolo Blasucci at Frosinone," November 4, 1776, *Letters of Saint Alphonsus Maria de Liguori,* V. III, p. 172.

3. St. Alphonsus Liguori, "To Father Angelo Maione at Naples," *Letters of Saint Alphonsus Maria de Liguori,* V. III, p. 237.

4. St. Alphonsus Liguori, "To Father N. in the House of Scifelli," *Letters of Saint Alphonsus Maria de Liguori,* V. III, p. 143.

5. Austin Berthe, V. II, p. 423.

6. St. Alphonsus Liguori, "To Father Pietro Paolo Blasucci in the House at Frosinone," *Letters of Saint Alphonsus Maria de Liguori,* V. III, p. 156.

7. Austin Berthe, V. II, p. 434.

8. Austin Berthe, V. II, p. 434.

9. Austin Berthe, V. II, p. 440.

10. Austin Berthe, V. II, p. 441.

11. St. Alphonsus Liguori, "To Father Francesco Antonio de Paola at Frosinone," *Letters of Saint Alphonsus Maria de Liguori,* V. III, p. 294.

12. St. Alphonsus Liguori, "To Father Angelo Maione at Naples," April 12, 1779, *Letters of Saint Alphonsus Maria de Liguori*, V. III, p. 296.

13. St. Alphonsus Liguori, "To Father Mattia Bartolomeo Corrado at Ciorani," *Letters of Saint Alphonsus Maria de Liguori,* V. III, p. 306.

14. St. Alphonsus Liguori, "To Father Bartolomeo Corrado," *Letters of Saint Alphonsus Maria de Liguori,* V. III, p. 323.

15. St. Alphonsus Liguori, "To Father Antonio Tannoia at Iliceto," *Letters of Saint Alphonsus Maria de Liguori,* V. III, p. 324.

16. Austin Berthe, V. II, p. 482.

17. Austin Berthe, V. II, p. 479-480.

18. St. Alphonsus Liguori, "To Father Bartolomeo Mattia Corrado at Naples," *Letters of Saint Alphonsus Maria de Liguori,* V. III, p. 330.

19. St. Alphonsus Liguori, "To Father Angelo Maione at Naples," March 30, 1780, *Letters of Saint Alphonsus Maria de Liguori,* V. III, p. 337.

20. Austin Berthe, V. II, p. 485.

21. St. Alphonsus Liguori, "To Father Amelio Fioccelli at Frosinone," *Letters of Saint Alphonsus Maria de Liguori,* V. III, p. 352.

22. Quoted in Raimundo Tellería, Tomo II, p. 673.

23. Raimundo Tellería, Tomo II, p. 674.

24. Quoted in Austin Berthe, V. II, pp. 500-501.

25. St. Alphonsus Liguori, "To Father Pietro Paolo Blasucci at Girgenti," *Letters of Saint Alphonsus Maria de Liguori,* V. III, p. 368.

26. Raimundo Tellería, Tomo II, p. 674.

27. Raimundo Tellería, Tomo II, pp. 674-675.

28. Austin Berthe, V. II, p. 514.

29. St. Alphonsus Liguori, "To Father Bartolomeo Mattia Corrado," *Letters of Saint Alphonsus Maria de Liguori,* V. III, p. 438.

30. Raimundo Tellería, Tomo II, p. 679.

31. Raimundo Tellería, Tomo II, p. 681.

32. Austin Berthe, V. II, p. 493.

33. Austin Berthe, V. II, p. 577.

34. Austin Berthe, V. II, p. 582.

35. Raimundo Tellería, Tomo II, p. 738.

36. Austin Berthe, V. II, p. 592.

37. Austin Berthe, V. II, p. 592.

38. Raimundo Tellería, Tomo II, p. 742.

39. Raimundo Tellería, Tomo II, p. 745.

40. Austin Berthe, V. II, p. 697.